Other Books in the
Bucket to Greece Series

Chapter 1

A Delayed Flight

Bucket," Barry guessed, his voice dripping with complete indifference, reflecting the bored expression on his face.

"That cleaner has dipped her mop right back in the same bucket of slimy water so many times it must be filthy by now," I said, watching the woman swish the mucky mop around with as much enthusiasm as Barry and I had for our riveting game of 'I Spy'. "I hope she didn't skimp on the bleach."

V.D. BUCKET

"So is bucket the right answer or not?" Barry asked.

"No, try again," I told him.

"I'd rather not bother," Barry huffed, standing up to stretch. "Fancy another coffee?"

"We may as well, there's nothing else to do," I replied, drawing a mental map of all the possible toilet stops on the drive home, being positively awash with coffee at this point. "Just don't spill it on your sign this time, the cardboard is looking decidedly wilted."

Sticking his lower lip out Barry surveyed the sign with a furrowed frown. "The O has run into the U."

Having taken the precaution of arriving an hour early to be on the safe side, the two of us had been hanging around at the local airport which operated during the tourist season for a tedious five hours, waiting on the much delayed flight from Manchester. Barry was apprehensive enough as it was about meeting his potential in-laws for the first time without flashing a smudged and soggy cardboard sign, now reading Troot instead of Trout, in their direction.

We couldn't even alleviate the boredom with a spot of people watching, since the airport was practically deserted. It had been terribly remiss of us to fail to check on any delays before turning up.

"Any movement on the arrivals board yet, Barry?"

"Not a thing," Barry sighed. "How about we take a turn outside and get a breath of fresh air instead of coffee? I have the camera with me. This could be a good opportunity to get that last snap of me as a bachelor that Marigold has been nagging about."

Marigold had indeed been a nag on the subject, having already chosen the pride of place spot on our mantelpiece to display her brother's framed image.

"Save the film for the wedding," I advised. After five hours of sweat ridden anxiety Barry wasn't looking his best, though he would probably scrub up well for the wedding. "Anyway you don't want to risk taking any pictures here. Have you forgotten about that group of British anoraks who got arrested for espionage? They took photos at this very airport?"

"It had completely slipped my mind," Barry admitted, even though the airport was littered with prominent pictorial signs warning that taking photographs was strictly prohibited.

Barry probably wouldn't appreciate spending his wedding day locked in a dank damp cell with no running water, reduced to licking droplets of sweat from the concrete floor. I recalled one of the plane spotters comparing her stay in a Greek prison to a dungeon which she was forced to share with fifteen Albanians. Such a coterie of fellow convicts would do little to improve Barry's Greek language skills, though he may pick up a few words to make communication with Guzim a tad easier. As Barry's possible spell in a Greek cell flashed before my eyes I considered such a fate was probably moot anyway since he was unlikely to be locked up in a women's prison.

"Plane spotting strikes me as about exciting as Norman's hobby of collecting traffic cones. I've never really seen the appeal of plane spotting, have you?" Barry said.

"I haven't, but it ought to be in my blood considering I was almost fathered by an American fighter pilot based at Burtonwood during the war," I replied.

"An American fighter pilot certainly has a more glamorous ring to it than a dodgy soap salesman who'd gone AWOL," Barry chuckled.

"My paternity is no laughing matter," I protested, thinking it was bad enough that I had to endure the humiliation of being abandoned in a bucket as a baby at the railway station and saddled with the initials of V.D. with all their disease ridden connotations. "Anyway Violet Burke wasn't one hundred percent certain that it was the soap salesman who got her pregnant, she admitted she was a bit free with her favours."

"It would account for your obsession with hygiene," Barry interrupted.

"Come on, let's get that air," I said, hoping to distract Barry from the subject until I could extract more information from my mother during her imminent visit. I must admit to being more than a tad curious if the salesman, who had seduced Violet Burke before limping away on a probably fake lame leg, was still alive.

Stepping through the airport doors we were immediately enveloped in a blanket of suffocating heat. A taxi driver lounged against the boot of his cab, the engine running, the smoke from his cigarette filtering into the polluting mix of hydrocarbons belching from the vehicle's exhaust. Spotting our presence the taxi driver straightened up, gesticulating hopefully towards his vehicle. When we indicated we weren't in need of a cab he reverted back to his position of slumped indifference.

"That's Marigold again," I said as my mobile trilled. Answering the call I explained there was still no sign of the flight carrying our guests, expecting to receive yet another lecture on the wisdom of checking on flights before setting off to the airport. Instead of the anticipated lecture I received a request from my wife to pick up some milk before heading back.

"It is Sunday, all the shops in town are closed. Anyway milk would go off in this heat on the two-hour drive home. Spore-forming bacteria would turn it into a curdled spoiled mess and likely floor our guests with a nasty dose of food poisoning," I argued, wondering why my wife couldn't simply cross the village square to the local shop.

I was shocked when Marigold told me that the police, presumably acting on a tip-off that the law prohibiting Sunday opening was being wantonly flouted, had descended on the village shop, carting Despina away in handcuffs. I wondered which villager the shop keeper's mother had riled up enough to make them dob her in: the list of potential snitches was endless when one considered how many villagers the bitter woman had falsely maligned with baseless accusations of marital infidelity. Violet Burke would have to make do with a drop of tinned condensed milk in her tea.

"It's too hot out here," Barry complained. "I could kill for a shower."

"Well you'll have to get in line, once we get our guests back the queue for the bathroom will be six deep," I reminded him, relieved we were one less than expected since Cynthia was staying with Milton and Edna until the wedding.

"Perhaps Benjamin and Adam won't mind showering under Guzim's outside hosepipe, they may find it a novelty in the hot weather," Barry suggested.

"I rather think Guzim is treating the whole showering thing as even more of a novelty than usual, I practically get asphyxiated with the stench of chickens and rabbits unless I stand downwind of him," I said.

"Well he is making money from muck, you have to admire his initiative," Barry reminded me. "And you must admit he's got the magic touch when it comes to the clutch of chickens you're rearing."

"He certainly has, we're knee-deep in eggs. Ah, some sign of action at last," I said, perking up at the sight of two tourist coaches pulling into the airport car park.

"They must be here to pick up the arrivals," Barry said, pointing out the blatantly obvious. Recognising the woman stepping down from a coach as the jumped up jobsworth who was technically still my supervisor at the holiday company I worked for on a part-time basis, I ducked out of sight. She was hard to miss in the Tango orange uniform that clashed with her cheap fake tan, but I had no desire to run into Tiffany on my day off.

"Let's give the arrivals board another scan," Barry suggested.

The arrivals area was finally showing signs of life when we returned inside. Uniformed check-in staff ambled over to man the passport control desks and holiday reps filtered in, leaving sandy footprints on the sloppily mopped floor.

"It's due to land any minute," I said, excited at the prospect of reuniting with my son Benjamin and his life-partner Adam. Even though Benjamin had reacted with delight to the discovery that he had a long lost granny, I was curious how he'd managed to endure Violet Burke in close proximity during the long flight over.

Barry, having never met the prospective in-laws he was due to collect, appeared more nervous than excited. Cynthia had made it clear that her parents could be judgmental and Barry was worried he may not live up to their high expectations. Grabbing his cardboard sign he held it aloft in readiness, even though the plane had only just touched down and the passengers were yet to disembark.

"Relax Barry, you're marrying Cynthia, not her parents," I advised.

"I just wish Cynthia could have been here to break the ice, rather than working today," Barry sighed.

"Stop worrying, it's hot enough to melt any ice and Cynthia will have finished work by the time you get them back to Meli. They'll likely be so frightened of the hair-pin bends on the drive back that you'll be spared an interrogation."

The passengers began to descend from the plane and make their way across the concourse, lining up to file through passport control. As they spilled into the arrivals lounge and baggage collection their mood appeared to be a mix of excited relief at having finally landed and weary disgruntlement at the four hour delay marring the start of their vacation.

"This could be them," Barry hissed as a

well-dressed couple headed in our direction, only to be rudely elbowed aside by an overdone bulbous woman with a shock of garishly dyed red hair bulldozing her way through. I braced myself in case Violet Burke decided to clamp me to her bosom in a suffocating embrace. I needn't have worried; it appeared my mother was not one for public displays of affection, though she clearly had no reservations about very loud and vocal public displays of complaint.

"I tell you that flight was a nightmare Victor, an absolute bane. Eight hours we've been stuck in that stuffy tin can with wings, have you seen how squashed up the seats are? Not a bit of leg or elbow room and I could barely squeeze my backside into the loo. And as for that plastic stuff they call food. I wish I'd packed those tins of Spam in my hand luggage."

Being tall I could sympathise with my mother; she is certainly a woman of stature and budget seats are notoriously uncomfortable. Nevertheless I found it a tad embarrassing that she voiced her complaints so vociferously, attracting bemused stares.

Before I could get a word in edgeways Violet Burke continued, "It shouldn't be allowed, they should have just knocked that hysterical harpy out instead of indulging her and inconveniencing everyone else. They made us sit on the runway for four hours after they finally carted her off the plane."

Barry and I exchanged puzzled glances. It sounded as though the flight had been delayed by the antics of an unruly passenger.

"Well you're here now, what have you done with Benjamin and Adam?" I asked.

"They're getting the suitcases."

"Would you like to sit down while we wait?"

"I've been stuck in a seat for so long that my backside is numb and all the blood had sunk to my feet, look how my ankles are all swelled up," Violet Burke said.

"You should have walked round on the plane to ease the swelling," I advised.

"There wasn't room to swing a cat." My mother's words conjured an unfortunate image of her attempting to swing a feline mid-flight over the heads of her fellow passengers.

"Let's find you a seat so you can elevate your feet to reduce the puffiness while we wait for the boys," I suggested, worried by the bulging flesh strangulated by wrinkled nylon threatening to explode from her flat lace-up shoes.

"I'll just wait here, I don't want to miss the in-laws," Barry said peering around anxiously. Flexing his arms he held the sign higher, his weary expression making it appear as though the sign was fashioned out of concrete rather than cardboard. Spotting two familiar figures heading towards me weighed down with cases I rushed forward to greet Benjamin and Adam, hoping my public paternal embraces didn't make them cringe with embarrassment.

"You're finally here," I said with a smile.

"We missed our slot with all the kerfuffle at Manchester, at least we knew you'd have the sense to check if there were any delays before setting off to meet us," Benjamin said. "Imagine how awful it would have been if you'd been waiting around here for four hours."

"Five actually, we didn't want to be late," I admitted. "What was the hold-up? Violet Burke said something about an unruly passenger."

"Not unruly as such, a woman let her fear of flying get the better of her and had to be escorted from the plane," Adam explained. "As a flight attendant I've see many cases of aviophobia, but never one so extreme as this. The woman was a gibbering wreck from the moment the doors closed. I think the pilot made the right call having her booted off before her panic became contagious."

"It certainly sounds like a case of extreme anxiety," I said, adding my concern about her well-being once she was removed from the flight.

"Well her husband got off with her so she wasn't alone," Benjamin said.

"And how was it flying over with Violet Burke?" I asked.

"When Granny got a bit much we just put our in-flight headphones on to drown her out," Benjamin said. "She got a few nasty looks when she started carping on about the fear-of-flying passenger being a wimpish blob of jelly ruining the start of everyone's holiday, but after we'd been sitting on the runway for four hours going nowhere I think most of the other passengers were so fed up that they agreed with her."

"Let's see if her swollen ankles have de-flated yet," I suggested, leading the boys over to where Violet Burke was seated, the last few stragglers dragging their suitcases past us.

Chapter 2

Smuggling Lard

Why is Uncle Barry holding a sign saying Troot?" Benjamin queried. "Is he moonlighting as a taxi driver?"

"It's supposed to read Trout. He's waiting for Cynthia's parents, they were on your flight," I replied.

"It doesn't look like it, there's no one left to come through," Adam pointed out. We had waited so long for Violet Burke's feet to deflate that it appeared everyone from the flight had already exited arrivals.

"Perhaps they didn't notice him and are waiting outside," Benjamin said.

Cynthia's description of her parents fitted almost every late middle- aged couple that had just passed through the airport. Barry was beginning to hyperventilate, convinced he had somehow missed the Trouts. Mislaying his prospective in-laws in a foreign country was hardly likely to be well received by his fiancée, particularly one prone to bridezilla moments. I pondered the likelihood of Cynthia having a Lady Bracknell moment and accusing Barry of carelessness in losing two of her parents, before ruling it out. Cynthia tended to favour dog- eared chick-lit left in the coastal book swaps that passed as the nearest thing to a public library, rather than the classics.

"Keep calm Barry, I'll do a quick recce outside and see if I can spot any likely looking candidates," I told him, wondering if the Trouts were perhaps mingling in with the crush for the coaches.

A sudden thought struck me. I recalled Cynthia recounting that due to her mother's morbid fear of flying her parents had never ventured abroad before. Not wishing to alarm Barry unless my hunch was confirmed I asked Adam to do a quick check with someone from the airline to see if the Trouts had been the couple escorted from the plane.

Hoisting herself up Violet Burke joined me as I stepped outside, complaining that if the customs officials back in Manchester hadn't confiscated the block of lard she'd had in her handbag she would have been able to rub it into her swollen feet. My mind boggled at the absurdity of her attempting to smuggle lard to the land of olive oil. Closing my eyes to blank out the gross image of her lard smeared swollen feet I ran slap-bang into Tiffany, almost knocking her over. The hand I reached out to steady her recoiled at the touch of damp polyester, the cheap sweaty cloth no doubt a veritable petri dish of multiplying germs.

"Oh Victor, I didn't like know you were at the airport. Grab a trolley to like help that old couple with their cases? You have to get them on like coach number two sharpish, we're already late for the off and with this like delay the customer satisfaction surveys will be like horrible," Tiffany barked in full-on jobsworth mode.

"It may have escaped your notice Tiffany

but I'm not actually on airport duty. If you'd checked the rotas you would have seen I have this week off."

"Surely you can lug like a few cases…" Tiffany began, before Violet Burke interrupted.

"Who do you think you are bossing him around? You young'uns need to show a bit of respect for the old folk? You can hardly expect anyone to take you seriously when you're sweating all over that ghastly orange nylon uniform."

I visibly cringed as my mother so casually lumped me in with the old folk. I could handle Tiffany perfectly well without my mother's interference, considering it was over fifty years late. I reflected that the old harridan would certainly have come in very handy when Derek Little was stealing my marbles and threatening to snatch my lunch money: just to clarify that was back in my short trouser school days and well before my growth spurt. I cringed at the memory, recalling Derek Little certainly didn't live up to his name. Fortunately by the time I was eleven I towered over him and took my revenge with a Bunsen burner, though I'm not proud to admit it.

Tiffany visibly bristled, her face reddening

even more than usual. Her scant customer service skills flew out of the window as she pointedly ignored Violet Burke, instead loudly commiserating with me that I'd been "like hijacked by such a ghastly old bag on your like day off."

"That ghastly old bag happens to by my mother," I blurted out, thankful that Violet Burke was too engrossed in grappling a luggage trolley out of the hands of a terrified looking couple to have heard my comment. I'm sure that if Tiffany hadn't already been so red in the face she would have had the grace to blush; instead her mouth just fell open as she demonstrated her bewildered goldfish routine. I'm sure my own gawping features mirrored the reps when it suddenly struck me that for the first time ever I had publically acknowledged that I was related to Violet Burke.

"Well done for getting hold of a luggage trolley Granny," Benjamin called out, oblivious to the cowering couple who'd had the trolley so rudely snatched from their grasp. "Adam's had confirmation; it was Cynthia's mother who had the screaming abdabs on the plane. It's probably best if Uncle Barry hears it from you Dad. Hold on Granny, let me see to your cases, you'll give yourself a hernia."

BUCKET TO GREECE (VOL. 5)

* * * *

"Well that's that then, Cynthia is sure to cancel the wedding," Barry groaned.

"Get a grip lad, it's not as though you lost the Troots," Violet Burke snapped.

"It's the Trouts actually," Barry corrected, slinging the bedraggled cardboard sign into the nearest bin.

"Cynthia is hardly likely to blame you for her mother's breakdown and from everything she's said the wedding will probably go off much smoother without them," I assured Barry.

"It's not too late to change your mind about marrying her," Violet Burke interjected. "Like mother, like daughter, and if you'd seen the manic way her mother was carrying on earlier you'd be wise to have second thoughts."

"Mother, I think you should keep your opinions to yourself," I hissed.

"Well I was just saying. After all if he ditches her at the altar I won't need to waste those lovely tins of Spam on their wedding present."

"But then that gorgeous new hat you bought for the wedding would go to waste Granny," Benjamin said.

The expression on the old harridan's face slipped from battle-axe to doting grandma. Benjamin certainly had the knack of winding Violet Burke around his little finger.

"I suppose I'd better telephone Cynthia with the news that her parents aren't coming," Barry said dolefully.

"On the off-chance that they haven't already phoned her with the news I think it would be better if you told her in person," I advised. "Come on let's make a move."

"I'll go back with Barry to keep him company, best if he doesn't drive back alone," Adam volunteered. His thoughtful gesture was well received, though I surmised ulterior motives, suspecting Adam wasn't as besotted with his grandma-in-law-to-be as his boyfriend was.

It was already dark when we reached Meli, our guests having enjoyed a sunset so spectacular as we drove over the mountain road that even Violet Burke had been lost for words for once. The gleam of fairy lights on the roof terrace indicated that Marigold and Cynthia were waiting for us on high, an erroneous assumption that was belied by Marigold practically dragging Benjamin from the car the moment I braked and smothering him in motherly embraces. I noticed Cynthia hovered anxiously clutching the vile mutant cat to her bosom as Barry parked, apparently not in a rush to greet her parents. When Barry and Adam stepped out of the car and it was clear there were no other passengers, Cynthia rushed forward, saying "Barry, did you drop my parents at the hotel on the coast already? Surely they weren't so tired by the journey that they didn't want to come up to Meli to see me?"

"They didn't make it to Greece Cyn, I'm sorry. Your mother had a panic attack on the plane and had to be escorted off."

"That's putting it mildly, she was screaming so loudly anyone would have thought she was being murdered," Violet Burke interjected.

It struck me as odd that Cynthia's parents hadn't already telephoned her to break the news that they would be no-shows at her wedding: I gave them the benefit of the doubt and hoped their excuse for disappointing her was that Mrs Trout had needed to be sedated and was still too out of it to pick up a telephone.

Cynthia's bottom lip quivered as she received the news, robotically repeating "My parents aren't coming, they aren't coming."

"Come inside for a drink to steady your nerves," Barry urged.

Once we were all indoors Marigold poured celebratory drinks from a plastic bottle of supermarket plonk to welcome our houseguests. Wincing at the sour taste, Cynthia downed her glass in one, before hiccupping.

"Oh Barry, what are we to do? Do you think we should cancel the wedding and get married in England?"

"There's no need to overact Cyn, everything is arranged for us to tie the knot on Thursday. I'm done with England and all my family and our friends are here in Greece."

"And I spent good money on a new hat, not to mention a fancy wedding gift," Violet Burke butted in from the kitchen where she was peering into the cupboards. "Haven't you got anything proper to drink Victor, this wine is nastier than the vinegar we use in the chippy?"

Having honed in on the Metaxa, Violet Burke poured herself and Cynthia generous measures, saying "Get that down you girl and stop your snivelling, it will put hairs on your chest."

The alcohol was obviously hitting the spot. After downing the brandy Cynthia succumbed to another bout of hiccups, before giggling. "A hairy chest wouldn't be a good look; my wedding dress is a bit low-cut."

"So you are going to wear it on Thursday?" Barry asked hopefully.

Cynthia hesitated before replying. "But there will be no one to give me away."

It crossed my mind that the decent thing to do would be to step into the breach and offer to give Cynthia away, but after promising Barry I would be his best man I couldn't in all conscience let him down. Instead I proposed the next best thing, saying "I'm sure Milton would be proud to do it."

Chapter 3

Sensitive Peas

O ur visitors were ravenous after their journey. I suggested that the seven of us stroll along to the taverna once our guests had unpacked since the sandwiches that Marigold had prepared earlier had curled in the heat and the salad needed to be binned because Cynthia's vile mutant cat was caught giving it a good licking. Expecting Violet Burke to protest that she'd rather stay in the house and throw a tin of Fray Bentos steak and kidney in the oven than eat foreign muck, I was pleasantly surprised when she acquiesced to joining us without putting up a fight.

Marigold earned a withering look when she warned Violet Burke that it was necessary to take precautions before stepping outside.

"There's no need to imply I'm a bit loose just because there was a bit of a mix up over Victor's paternity," my mother snapped.

Not instantly catching Violet Burke's drift, Marigold looked a tad flummoxed; it had obviously never occurred to her to advise a woman in her late seventies to take the kind of precautions more associated with the prevention of spawning unwanted buckets.

"Precautions against mosquitoes," Marigold clarified as the penny dropped. "If you're anything like Victor you will be a magnet for the pesky blood suckers."

My mother announced that she had arrived well prepared, having knocked up an effective homemade repellent by combining tea tree and coconut oil as recommended by one of her chip shop regulars with a propensity for holidaying in mosquito infested countries.

"Can you spare a dab for me Vi?" Adam asked. "Coconut oil is so good for the skin."

"Well I didn't bother with the coconut bit,

have you seen the outrageous price?"

"So it's a blend of tea tree oil and...?"

"Well there was plenty of oil going begging in the chippy fryers."

We all took a collective step back as Violet Burke liberally slathered herself in the home-made repellent, the distinctive smell of stale chips announcing the second ingredient.

"You and Barry should go well together, he walks around doused in vinegar," I observed, scrumpling my nose as I caught a whiff of my mother.

"At least I'm bite free," Barry huffed, staring meaningfully at the latest itchy red blotch adorning my forehead.

"I think you smell very manly," Cynthia hiccupped, draping herself over her fiancé and tossing her glossy hair in his face. She was a tad tipsy and unsteady on her feet from the combination of cheap plonk and Metaxa.

"So are we going out to eat or what? I'm starved enough to eat a scabby horse," Violet Burke declared. "Is it the same taverna you dragged me to last time I was here?"

"Indeed, there's just the one in the village."

"I'd better grab a pair of Marigolds and some Vim them, the state of their lavvy was shocking."

With Violet Burke's head safely stuck under the sink as she searched for cleaning supplies, the rest of us engaged in a bout of collective eye rolling. The irony of a woman who freely slathered herself in stagnant oil from a chip shop fryer being obsessed with hygiene wasn't lost on us. Even Cynthia's vile mutant cat wasn't tempted to lick off the slick of oil, no doubt deterred by the scummy bits of old batter.

Arriving at the taverna I steered our group of seven to an outside table. The few low-wattage lights strung up outside provided little illumination and Violet Burke immediately complained that she'd never be able to see what she was eating in the dark. I was just relieved that she hadn't seen the spit and sawdust state of inside; standards of cleanliness had definitely dropped since I stopped cheffing there.

It was Nikos' first time meeting Adam and he greeted him with a bone crushing handshake before rushing inside to grab his wife and make the introductions. Dina made a big fuss over both boys. Even though neither of them could understand a word she said her genuine affection was evident. The previous wariness that had kept Dina and Violet Burke at a distance receded a little, my mother seemingly approving of anyone who so openly welcomed her grandson.

I was relieved to hear Nikos was planning to throw chicken on the grill since I considered *souvlaki* may be a tad too exotic for my mother's tastes. She had already caused consternation by demanding the chips and cheese were served without of any of that revolting green stuff that topped them on her last visit, oregano definitely falling under the far-reaching umbrella of ghastly foreign muck.

Tucking into the crusty bread, Cynthia began to sober up. I took the opportunity to remind her of my suggestion that Milton give her away on her wedding day, after all time was running out if she expected to find a stand-in for four days hence. Cynthia blushed before conspiratorially hissing to everyone at the table "I'm not sure Milton is a good choice, I'm finding it a bit difficult to look him in the eye at the moment. It's all very embarrassing."

"But Milton's a solid old chap..." Barry began to protest. "He never embarrassed you before you went to stay there, don't tell me he's been making unwanted advances."

The mental image of a frisky Milton limping along the landing clad in slippers and pyjamas that sprang to mind was dispelled when my mother revealed, "I've had plenty of unwanted advances in my time, as well as some wanted ones."

"Oh heavens no, nothing like that. This is going to come as a shock to you all…" Cynthia said, pausing for dramatic effect. "Milton has been writing a pornographic novel. He's not had it published yet but he suggested I flick through his manuscript of 'Delicious Desire' if I fancied a racy bedtime read, he said he would value my opinion."

"Actually Milton prefers to consider it erotica rather than porn," I said.

The look of shocked disbelief transforming Barry's face showed he was clueless about Milton's literary pursuit. "You knew about it Victor?"

"Oh we both did, we can never quite keep our faces straight when we imagine Edna as his muse," Marigold said, attempting to suppress a bout of laughter.

"You might have let me in on it," Barry grumbled, looking a tad put out that he'd been left out of the loop.

"I'm sure I mentioned it to you discreetly, perhaps you weren't listening. Anyway we didn't think that Milton intended for it to become public knowledge, after all he is penning it under a pseudonym," I protested, thinking it best if I avoiding publically outing him as Scarlett Bottom.

"Like your book then," Barry blurted, immediately covering his mouth as the realisation hit him that he had just tactlessly divulged my secret. My brother-in-law swore under his breath, wiping away the droplets of sweat that dripped from his forehead down to his loose lips.

"Victor, you're writing porn," my mother accused.

"Of course I'm not doing any such thing. I am writing a book about our experiences moving to Greece," I admitted. "There is nothing remotely smutty about it."

"But you have to keep it under your hats, I would never live it down if word got out. I'm not having Victor turning us into a pair of laughing stocks," Marigold insisted, subjecting everyone at the table to one of her withering looks.

"So you'll be using a discreet pen name?"

Benjamin asked.

"Yes, I'm dusting off the old Bucket name," I confirmed.

"Bucket?" Cynthia queried.

"I'll fill you in on it later," Barry told her, before turning to me and shrugging apologetically. "Cynthia is about to become a member of the family."

"So my son is going to be a famous writer," Violet Burke said. I think I detected a hint of pride in my mother's voice, but Marigold was still determined to distance herself from any literary fame I may attract.

"He won't be famous if I've got anything to do with it, Vi. He's using the Bucket pen name to remain anonymous."

"I suppose if he went with Blossom it might be a bit of a giveaway," Violet Burke said.

"Granny's maiden name," Benjamin explained to everyone who was looking confused.

"I'd never have guessed you were a budding writer Victor," Cynthia said. "It is Marigold who is always scribbling away in a notebook."

"Oh that's nothing, I just like to keep a diary," Marigold said modestly, blushing profusely and avoiding my eye. I considered she needn't blush on my account: it would never occur to me to invade my wife's privacy by peeking into her diary, even though I would like to satisfy my curiosity regarding the amount of superfluous exclamation marks she actually littered the pages with.

"I can see why Cynthia doesn't want a paid up member of the dirty mac brigade giving her away," Violet Burke interjected.

"You've got totally the wrong impression Mother," I replied. "Milton is a lovely old gent who is dabbling in writing erotica to make a bit of cash after falling on hard times."

"I've certainly never seen Milton in a raincoat," Cynthia said, her denseness indicating she had taken my mother's dirty mac comment a bit too literally. "Still, I think it could be a bit awkward if he gave me away, I'd hate to break into laughter midway through my vows. Every time I imagine Milton writing his raunchy 'Delicious Desire' it sets me off."

"How about asking Nikos to give you away then?" I suggested, thinking Nikos had a commanding presence and would be able to reign in Cynthia quite smoothly if she had a bridezilla meltdown on the big day.

"That's not a bad idea at all, I wonder if he'd

be up for it?" Cynthia replied.

"There's only one way to find out," I said.

"I'll pop into the kitchen and ask him now," Cynthia said with enthusiasm.

"Hold on a sec," Violet Burke said. Rummaging around in her enormous handbag she produced a Tupperware dish. "Tell him to heat these mushy peas up while you're there, they'll go well with the chicken and chips."

As Cynthia disappeared inside a bemused Barry leaned in close. "Milton's a bit of a dark horse; I'd never have guessed what he's been up to. I'm genuinely sorry I let it slip out about your book Victor."

"Do try to be less indiscreet in future," I advised. "It will probably come to nothing anyway, what with one thing and another I've barely a free moment to get creative."

The locals began to arrive, casting curious glances at our group as they settled at their tables. Having only ventured into the taverna once during her previous visit Violet Burke was an unknown to most of the locals, and of course as this was Adam's first visit to Meli he was a complete novelty. Panos wandered over to reacquaint himself with Benjamin, having reluctantly accepted that my son's sexual orientation ruled him out as a possible suitor for his grand-daughter.

"*Einai oti o filos*?" he said, asking if Adam was the boyfriend.

"*Einai etairoi tis zois*," I replied, clarifying the boys were life partners. I would have liked to explain that if ever gay marriage was legalised I would be proud to welcome Adam as my son-in-law: however it had been a long day and the necessary Greek words were too taxing for my brain to cope with.

Panos barely appeared to hear my reply. With his attention fully focused on Violet Burke, he said, "*kai afti i omorfi ynaika*?" asking who the fine looking woman was.

"*Einai i matera mou*," I replied, publically admitting for the second time that day that Violet Burke was my mother.

"*Afti i omorfi ynaika*," Panos repeated, shuffling nervously in his wellies. It struck me that Panos appeared to have absolutely no recollection of my mother bursting into the chicken curry dinner party we had hosted the previous year, a memorable event that would forever be etched on my brain because it was my first ever encounter with the woman who had so callously abandoned me in a bucket. Recalling that I had stormed out of the house following my mother's arrival I considered perhaps Panos hadn't stuck around for long enough after my departure for her presence to register. He had no reason to consider the moment as memorable as I did, but Violet Burke was undoubtedly a formidable statuesque figure who was hard to forget. Hoping that Panos wasn't coming down with the same affliction shared by Spiros' Uncle Leo and Marigold's late Aunty Beryl, I recalled he had been a tad preoccupied since parting with the sheep that had stalked the village after losing its libido.

My ruminations were interrupted by Nikos yelling for me to join him in the kitchen. Sometimes my former boss appeared to harbour the delusion I was still skivvying for him, but nevertheless I headed inside, wondering why he sounded so irate. Dina, a broad smile on her face was hugging an equally smiley Cynthia in a motherly embrace, so Nikos' show of temper didn't appear to be related to the request to give Cynthia away.

"Victor, I not to care if the woman is the family of you. You cannot to allow her to bring in this inferior shop bought food, I will not to

stand it," Nikos bellowed, pointing at the Tupperware box of mushy peas my mother had retrieved from the depths of her handbag.

"Well technically they aren't shop bought
because my mother brought them from the chip
shop where she works," I protested weakly. I
was naturally reluctant to make false claims
since I was uncertain if the peas were out of a
tin, thus originally shop bought, or prepared in
the chippy from soaking dried legumes: not
wishing to be a pedant they would actually be
homemade if the latter.

"The chip shop?" Nikos queried.

"Yes indeed, a chip shop is a British institu-
tion much like a Greek taverna in its long-stand-
ing traditions. They cook fish, similar to Dina's
bakaliaros, with chips. Instead of serving *skordalia*
with fish and fried potatoes, it comes with
mushy peas," I explained.

"Curry sauce is becoming increasingly popular though," Cynthia interrupted.

"What is this, the mushy?" Nikos demanded, ignoring the reference to curry.

"Hold on a sec and I'll look it up," I said,
flipping through the pages of my handy English
to Greek dictionary which I'd got in the habit of
taking along with me to the taverna. I knew

from experience that one never knew when one could be caught short of a necessary Greek word.

"Mushy, are here we are, in Greek the word is *evaisthitos*. So it must be *evaisthitos arakas*," I said, adding the Greek word for peas.

Nikos stared at me as though I'd taken leave of my senses. "Victor you talk the nonsense."

"Isn't *evaisthitos* the Greek word for sensitive?" Cynthia butted in. "Nikos is right, sensitive peas does sound like nonsense. Niko, how would we say 'slow cooked peas' correctly?"

"*Arga mageiremena bizelia*," Nikos replied, the familiar twinkle returning to his eyes.

"Anyway she brought them over with her from England, she didn't buy them in the local shop," I explained, aware I was being punctilious.

"No one could to buy the anything in the shop when the police arrest the Despina," Nikos said before relenting and telling me that Violet Burke could have her sensitive peas if I was prepared to heat them up myself. Anything for a quiet life I thought. Joining Dina in the kitchen I teased her that she needn't get any ideas I was there to chop onions or fry chips.

"So did Nikos agree to give you away?" I

asked Cynthia as I stirred the peas.

A look of pride suffused Nikos' handsome features as he declared "I am the honoured," before heading back to the grill.

Chapter 4

No Siren Temptress

I am so pleased that Nikos has agreed to give me away," Cynthia said as we tucked into delicious grilled chicken and Dina's legendary chips. "He is going to have a word with the mayor and ask if we can have the ceremony in the fancy room at the *Dimarcheio*, rather than just signing the register in a cramped office. It will make it so much more special."

"I know the room you mean, the door was ajar when I went to meet the mayor," I said, not bothering to elaborate that my initial foray into local politics had been nothing but a wild goose chase because all the important local dignitaries had been off gadding at a funeral. "It had a dais and seating, it would certainly add a formal touch to the occasion."

"We don't want something too solemn, perhaps we could fill it with flowers," Cynthia suggested.

"Oh, do let us arrange the flowers," Adam offered, exchanging an excited glance with Benjamin and squeezing his hand.

"Hopefully a fancy room with floral arrangements will make up for your parents' absence," Barry said, attempting to hide his relief that he wouldn't have to try to impress his new in-laws. Spooning some mushy peas onto his plate he deftly changed the subject. "I say, these are a bit of all right, Vi."

"Don't let Nikos spot you eating those peas, he was very reluctant to allow them table room," I advised, discreetly covering my own dollop of mushy peas with a paper napkin. "Nikos rather frowns on food that wasn't invented by Greeks or that ever had shelf room in a shop."

"He should give them a try, he doesn't know what he's missing," Barry enthused.

I reflected that Nikos was unlikely to agree. Our Greek host had to date sneered at both tartare and mint sauce as vile concoctions that couldn't compare to *skordalia* or a squeeze of fresh *lemoni*. My palate had embraced many recently discovered Greek flavours, yet I had to admit Violet Burke's mushy peas would have made me nostalgic for the odd chippy dinner from a scrupulously hygienic establishment if I hadn't perfected homemade *bakaliaros* and *skordalia,* under Dina's excellent guidance; still there was no sense in deliberately antagonising Nikos.

As we shared the meal our talk turned to plans for the coming fortnight. Obviously the highlight of the week would be Barry and Cynthia's wedding on Thursday. Apart from the day out on Pegasus I hadn't arranged anything specific for our visitors. I considered that presenting them with an itinerary might make their visit resemble one of the organised excursions I led. I had no intention of blowing my whistle to keep my houseguests in order; after all they were on holiday, not in a boot camp. Our guests agreed that after the rigours of travel they would appreciate nothing more taxing than lounging about the next day, relaxing in the garden and perhaps exploring the hidden walkways in the village.

"I do wish I could join you all on the boat trip on Tuesday, but I don't finish work until Wednesday afternoon," Cynthia lamented.

"But when you return to work after your break you will be in charge of the office and the ghastly Tiffany will be gone," I reminded her.

"I hope I can cope with the promotion on top of the move. Barry and I will be very busy getting Harold's house sorted out as soon as we're married," Cynthia said. I sensed a note of panic in her voice as she explained to our English guests that they would be receiving the keys to their new home on their wedding day. Although Barry wouldn't be tackling his planned renovations immediately they would still need to get the house cleaned and furnished before they could live in anything resembling comfort.

Leaning in, Marigold whispered, "Victor, Cynthia is beginning to look decidedly frazzled around the edges, she hasn't had a day off for ages. I think we should tell them about our surprise gift now." Looking over at Cynthia, I agreed. She was clearly stressed out by the idea of combining work with getting the new house in habitable order. I considered Marigold was right, Cynthia may well decompress if she knew there was a spot of relaxation on the horizon.

"Actually you won't be able to sort out the house right away, the pair of you will be too busy enjoying your mini-break honeymoon," I announced to Barry and Cynthia.

"I don't understand…" Cynthia said.

"Marigold and I are treating the two of you to a couple of nights away in a hotel after the wedding."

Immediately bursting into tears Cynthia grabbed an already soggy paper napkin to blow her nose, whilst Barry objected, saying our magnanimous gesture was too much, plus they really needed to make a start on sorting the house.

"Nonsense Barry, the two of you deserve a honeymoon," Marigold insisted. "Victor will take the keys off Harold and we can start sorting the house out for you on Friday. We'll roll up our sleeves and give it a thorough scrubbing. I'm sure the boys will be happy to lend a hand carting furniture over from our downstairs storage once the place is clean."

"Count us in," Benjamin and Adam selflessly volunteered.

"We can't expect you to give up a day of your holiday," Barry protested.

"Don't go looking a gift horse in the mouth Uncle Barry, we both have quite an eye for interior décor, we'll be in our element," Benjamin said firmly.

"I hope you have plenty of Vim in Victor, I like to get into every grimy corner, there's no telling how much muck has accumulated. That Joan struck me as a slovenly housekeeper," Violet Burke added, surprising us all with her ready willingness to muck in.

"It's very sporting of you all to offer to clean the place up, it will be brilliant to be able to move in knowing that all trace of Harold and Joan has been thoroughly eradicated," Barry said.

Between bouts of sobbing Cynthia gushed, "I couldn't ask for nicer in-laws, it's so generous of you both to arrange a honeymoon break, especially as you're already treating us to the wedding reception."

It was true we were already pulling out all the stops by paying for the reception, but having the do at Nikos' taverna would hardly make a dent in the bank balance, even though he had rashly promised to lay on canapés for the occasion. My thoughts were distracted by the familiar sting of a blood sucking mosquito feasting on my neck. As I slapped it away with a tad too much force for comfort, my mother wordlessly passed me her bottle of rancid repellent.

Abandoning the smokey grill, Nikos pulled out a chair and joined us, eager to share the latest gossip about the police raid on the village shop. He told us that Despina, the shop-keeper's mother, had been manning the shop alone when two police cars rolled up, sirens blaring. The unnecessary sirens appeared to be a calculated overblown ploy, intended to disturb the afternoon siesta and alert the villagers to the dramatic events about to unfold under their inquisitive noses.

"The police take the Despina away for opening the illegally on the Sunday," Nikos said. "I think the, how you say in English, the hand chains, were for the entertainment."

"Handcuffs," I corrected.

"That sounds a bit extreme, two cop cars to take away one cantankerous old busybody," Barry commented.

"But the handcuffs were a glorious touch," Marigold declared smugly, happy to have witnessed the drama. Although not catty by nature my wife had every right to gloat over Despina's humiliation. Only a day earlier the scandalmonger behind the counter had hinted to Marigold that it was inviting disaster to give houseroom to Cynthia since she was a younger model who would use all her feminine wiles to tempt me to be unfaithful. Although Marigold gave short shrift to such a ridiculous notion, secure in the knowledge I am a faithful and devoted husband who would never chase after another woman, Despina continued to imply I was some kind of sex-crazed philanderer.

"She break the law," Nikos insisted, his glowering expression conveying the impression that hanging, drawing and quartering the universally despised woman would be a suitable punishment for her slight misdemeanour.

"But I'm confused by the illegality, the shops on the coast open on Sundays," I said, recalling how Marigold had stocked up on cat food in a coastal supermarket on a recent Sunday.

"They maybe have the permit for the tourist shopping, or maybe they not. The police not to bother with the illegal opening unless the report is make about the law break. Someone in the village must to make the report against the Despina, she is not the well liked," Nikos said.

"I can't help speculating if Tina dobbed her own mother in just to get a break from the interfering hag," Marigold said. "It's quite clear her patience has worn thin having Despina in the shop so much lately. I've seen how Tina winces when Despina goes out of her way to insult the customers, it can't be good for business."

Marigold certainly had a point. Tina's wartfaced mother had only recently arrived in the village, her husband having run off with another woman. Whilst it was only natural that Tina wanted to offer support to her mother, she must be tearing her hair out over the loss of business, with loyal regulars shunning the village store rather than risk running the gauntlet of the bitter harridan's acidic tongue. It didn't particularly surprise me when Nikos revealed that Tina had re-opened the shop for illegal Sunday trading as soon as the police cars sped away. I presumed that Nikos must have had his own run-in with Despina since he appeared most put out that she would likely be able to bribe her way to freedom with a well-padded brown envelope.

The ears of one of the elderly local gents at the next table pricked up at the mention of Despina. Flinging his *komboloi* beads in a wild clattering gesture he swore aloud before ranting something in indecipherable Greek.

"The Grigoris say the Despina try to make much the trouble, she say to Grigoris' wife he visit the widow Litsa in the siesta hour to make the *kamaki*. The good is the wife told the Grigoris to take the bag of *horta* to the Litsa, she know he not make the *kamaki*, the evil tongue of the shop keeper stir the lies," Nikos said, standing up to tend to Litsa's brother Kostas who had just arrived.

"*Kamaki*?" Benjamin asked.

"The Greek art of reeling a woman in," I explained, "though I rather thought the term was restricted to courting foreign tourists. Spiros enjoyed engaging in a bit of *kamaki* before he met Sampaguita, though he didn't tend to be very successful at it."

"Well it's certainly all going on in this village," Adam said with obvious relish, being quite partial to a bit of juicy gossip. "I suppose this widow woman must be a bit of a temptress if the shopkeeper was trying to stir up marital trouble?"

Almost choking on his chicken Barry spluttered, "Litsa's a lovely old lady, but she's no siren temptress. She's barely five feet tall and as wrinkly as an old prune, mind you it's quite impressive the speed she can hobble through the village with the aid of her stick."

"She dotes on Barry, if Litsa was thirty years younger she'd be serious competition for Cynthia," Marigold joked, reaching over to ruffle Barry's hair atop his blushing face. Cynthia's suddenly sour expression made it clear she didn't appreciate Marigold's sense of humour.

From the corner of my eye I observed many of the locals approaching Kostas, placing reassuring hands on his shoulder and generally fussing about him as he held court. I wondered if something had happened to solicit such attention. My curiosity was satisfied when Eleni waddled over to clear the table, though she had a difficult job reaching it over her pregnant stomach. Pulling up a chair to briefly take the weight off her swollen ankles, Eleni confided that Matthias' sister Litsa had taken a nasty tumble and was currently confined to a hospital bed in town.

"Who is Matthias?" I asked in confusion.

"The old brother of Litsa," Eleni replied.

"But Cynthia said he was called Kostas...I had a feeling his name began with an M."

My remark was met with a disinterested

shrug

"Kostas, Matthias, it's all the same," Barry snapped before crying with genuine concern "it's just terrible about Litsa." A certain fondness had developed between my brother-in-law and the old lady who lived in the house opposite the taverna. Litsa clearly doted on Barry, forever showering him with homemade goodies; in turn he made a point of stopping by regularly and assisting with any odd jobs, brushing aside any mention of payment and blushing modestly when we teased him that he had an ancient admirer. "Did she break any bones?"

"She is shook up and bruised, but nothing is broken," Eleni said. "She stay in the *nosokomeio* for the doctor to observe."

"Is there anyone there with her now?" Barry asked, clearly worried she was alone since her brother was in the taverna.

We had learnt during our time in Greece that relatives tended to flock to the bed of hospitalised patients, performing the duties more usually associated with nurses. Indeed it was rather expected that whole families would camp out overnight by the hospital beds of their loved ones.

"Matthias has just got back from the hospital,

he will return again tomorrow, for the now Litsa has the niece by the bed, he come from Athens," Eleni revealed.

"Does she mean the nephew?" Benjamin hissed to me, clearly confused by Eleni referring to Litsa's niece as he.

"I think niece, Greeks often mix up English pronouns," I clarified. I had picked up on the peculiar quirk of even Greeks with an excellent mastery of English often confusing gender when speaking in a foreign language; I found it a tad surprising considering their own language seemed far more complicated than English, attributing genders to inanimate objects. At one point as I pored over my Greek text book I had begun to feel I had a handle on the subject, only to throw my book at the wall in frustration when I discovered all the genders I thought I had grasped changed again in the plural. Of course I didn't actually throw the book as that would have been a puerile gesture, but I was certainly tempted.

"I do hate to think of Litsa in the hospital, a nasty fall at her age could result in complications," Barry sighed, his face etched with concern. "Do you suppose I'd be allowed to visit her tomorrow?"

"Of course, it is the right thing to do," Eleni said. "Litsa only have the brother to live in Meli, Dina tell me most the family move to Athens."

"I don't suppose I could persuade you to come with me Victor? There's no way my builder's Greek is up to finding my way round a hospital," Barry pleaded.

"I can't guarantee my Greek is up to the job, but I'm willing to lend my support," I agreed, thinking it was high time I at least familiarised myself with the Greek healthcare system since we never knew when we may need it. I felt a slight twinge of guilt; if I was off gallivanting at the hospital it would leave Marigold responsible for entertaining Violet Burke.

"I do hope Litsa recovers in time for the wedding, I know how much she's been looking forward to a good knees-up," Barry said.

"We'll save her some canapés and cake," Cynthia suggested a tad unsympathetically, having never quite appreciated the way in which Litsa made such a fuss of her fiancé.

Chapter 5

Sweet Way to go Gay!

Not wishing to disturb our houseguests who would surely appreciate a lie-in following the tedium of their delayed travel, I silently crept from my bed before dawn, humming with anticipatory delight at the prospect of my morning dose of caffeine. The house was blissfully quiet, thus it took me completely by surprise when I discovered Barry sprawled out snoring on the sofa. His slumbering presence was unexpected because I'd presumed he would have sneaked over to Milton's house to share Cynthia's bed. I hoped that Cynthia had not succumbed to another bridezilla moment resulting in a lovers' tiff.

The delicious early morning breeze wafting in from the open balcony doors tempted me to step outside whilst I waited for the kettle to boil. Basking in the early silence I surveyed the sleeping village, watching as the buildings and trees emerged from darkness, gradually beginning to take solid form. I jumped in alarm when a speeding shape suddenly sprang out of nowhere, landing with a thud on the balcony, almost knocking me off balance. Sighing in frustration I realised that Cynthia's vile mutant tom must have returned from a night on the tiles, no doubt ravishing and pillaging its way through the cowering stray population of Meli. Grabbing it under one arm I deposited the foul creature outside the front door, knowing its presence would put Marigold's imported domestic felines off their breakfast.

Clawsome and Catastrophe crept out of hiding, secure in the knowledge that the predatory male monster had been given its marching orders. The pampered cats sidled up to me in the kitchen, brushing against my leg in a blatant display of faux affection. Aware I would have no more peace until their bowls were full I opened a tin of cat food, recoiling in disgust at the repulsive smell. I reflected that Marigold must have a cast iron stomach; goodness knows how she tolerated swallowing the stuff without retching during her career as a pet food taster. Pickles put in a late appearance, turning its nose up at the congealed jellied offering in the bowl, though I can't say I blamed it. Giving in to a moment of weakness I opened a tin of sardines for the kitten.

I cringed as the din of the electric coffee grinder pulverised the excellent Brazilian coffee beans, the noise reverberating loudly. I had no wish to waken the sleeping household since I relished the solitary enjoyment of drinking my first coffee whilst watching the sunrise. It would certainly have been quieter to settle for an *Ellinkos kafe* made from powder, but my stomach objected to such a rude awakening first thing in the morning. Stepping back out on the balcony I sipped my aromatic brew, the first rays of sunlight casting a mellow pink and blue glow over the sea on the horizon. The truly mesmerising view was one I knew I would never tire of.

The sound of clunky footsteps in the grand salon distracted my attention from the magnificent sunrise; it appeared that the racket from the coffee grinder had unfortunately disturbed my mother. Violet Burke headed towards the balcony, bizarrely wrapped up for the arctic depths of winter despite the heat of summer. I recognised the ugly fuchsia dressing gown that looked as though it had been hacked from an old candlewick bedspread, from her previous visit, but the addition of rollers poking out of a Hilda Ogden style head scarf was a novel addition. I reflected that the comparison was a tad unjust; my mother bore less of a resemblance to the Rovers Return charwoman than she did to the infamous Elsie Tanner. My mind wandered for a moment as I pondered if I was confusing Elsie Tanner with Ena Sharples; no matter, to the best of my recollection both soap opera icons were formidable northern women; no doubt Violet Burke would consider it a compliment to be lumped in with them.

Before I had the chance to wish my mother good morning or establish if she was indeed a Coronation Street fan, she started grouching, demanding to know what kind of house I was running to allow a naked man free reign in the garden.

"It's not the kind of thing I expect to confront

when I open the curtains, do you suppose he's one of those streakers after attention? I was tempted to chuck a bucket of water out of the window, but he was already wet."

Presuming my mother had suffered the misfortune of catching an eyeful of Guzim showering under the outside hosepipe, I reflected that she needn't act so affronted. I very much doubted that Guzim was flashing anything that she hadn't seen before, considering the number of husbands she had apparently gone through. Personally it came as a relief to hear that Guzim was actually washing since I was less likely to be asphyxiated by his chicken and rabbit stench when I ventured into the garden to remind him to bag up all the droppings. On the other hand if Guzim was showering today it struck me as unlikely that he would choose to indulge in further ablutions before the wedding, to which Barry had impulsively extended an invitation, much to Cynthia's chagrin.

Defending the Albanian shed dweller from my mother's contempt, I told her "I don't suppose he expected anyone to be up to witness him stripping off at this early hour."

"I suppose that figures. Marigold doesn't strike me as the type to be up with the lark. No doubt you pamper her with tea in bed…"

"Coffee actually, may I pour you one?"

"You can do me a mug of tea, but make sure it's strong enough for the spoon to stand up."

"Coming up," I promised, escaping to the kitchen. Searching through the cupboards I hoped that Marigold had managed to get hold of some PG Tips for our guest. I could just imagine the scathing reaction if I handed Violet Burke a cup of Earl Grey, my personal tea tipple of choice. We appeared to have an ample supply of said Earl Grey and *tsai tou vounou*, Greek mountain tea, in the cupboard, but I imagined that a mugful of twigs was unlikely to be well received. To my great relief I uncovered some PG Tips behind the stock of tinned cat food. Remembering we were out of milk I added a dollop of the condensed stuff to my mother's mug.

"Here this takes me back Victor, I don't think I've had condensed milk in my tea since rationing," Violet Burke gushed nostalgically. "It's funny how I got out of the habit once things returned to normal. October 53 it was when they lifted the tea rationing. It was like drinking cat's piss when supplies were short in the war. Of course I had my ways of getting hold of black market tea, but it wasn't regular."

"I remember when sweet rationing ended," I said. Casting my mind back to childhood I recalled standing in a seemingly endless queue at the corner shop, clutching the thruppence needed for a packet of fruity Spangles, desperately hoping I wouldn't get my hand on the prize only to have it viciously snatched away by Derek Little. I remember being desperate to taste my first Spangles, captivated by the colourful advertisement adorning the wall outside the railway station. I can still picture the poster now, an oblong packet of assorted fruit Spangles with the logo 'Sweet way to go gay!'

I reflected that they would never get away with an ad line like that these days, but I would share it later with Benjamin and Adam; knowing their sense of humour they would likely howl with laughter. The day that sweet rationing ending was certainly memorable, dare I say sweetly gay, in many ways; despite the rumblings of nausea in the pit of my stomach I can still recall the triumphant joy of having nothing but an empty wrapper from a packet of Spangles left by the time Derek Little finally caught up with me.

I decided it would be prudent not to share this memory with my mother since I wasn't quite sure how sensitive she was to passing references to railway stations. It wouldn't do to stir up possibly painful memories of abandoning me in a bucket, at least not before breakfast. There was one detail about my abandonment that still niggled. Violet Burke was such a stickler for hygiene that I couldn't understand why she hadn't bothered to scrub the coal dust from the bucket before dumping me in it. Surely she realised a grimy bonneted baby may not make a good first impression.

My ruminations were disturbed by a tap on the door. Hoping it wasn't Guzim at this early hour I slung the front door open to discover Cynthia drooling all over her vile mutant cat. I noted she looked remarkably fresh faced considering her lack of sobriety the previous evening.

"Is Barry still here?" Cynthia asked.

"Follow the sound of snoring. You'll find him on the sofa."

If Cynthia expected any form of privacy as she woke her fiancé with a tender kiss, she was out of luck. Violet Burke stood over the pair of them, noisily slurping her PG Tips. Rubbing the sleep from his bleary eyes Barry smiled at Cynthia, asking her if she had time for a coffee.

"I'm late already, I overslept," Cynthia apologised.

Running his fingers through Cynthia's glossy hair Barry said "I missed you."

"Fancy a coffee Barry?" I offered. "I must say it was a bit of a surprise to find you on the sofa."

"It didn't feel right sneaking into Milton's place last night; all the lights were out when I walked Cynthia back so I decided to crash here, let Cynthia catch up on her beauty sleep before the wedding."

"So much for my early night," Cynthia lamented. "I picked up Milton's manuscript to read in bed and before I knew it I was totally engrossed in 'Delicious Desire.'"

"Well I hope you didn't go getting any kinky ideas for our wedding night," Barry joked.

"I will never be able to look Edna in the eye again," Cynthia giggled. "It's going to be a bit awkward trying to avoid her when I've another three nights under their roof."

"Well if you've got any ideas about bunking in with me, you can forget them my girl," Violet Burke decreed, her steely glance brokering no argument.

"No, no, it's fine, it's only another three nights," Cynthia assured her, clearly intimidated by my mother. "I'll see you after work Barry?"

"How about we all meet up on the coast this evening and have dinner down there?" I suggested. "Barry and I aren't leaving for the hospital until after lunch and it may be a bit late for me to start cooking when we get back. If we go up to town in your van Barry then I can leave the Punto for Marigold to ferry our visitors."

"Sounds like a plan," Barry agreed.

"That Marigold has got a cushy life, leaving you to do the cooking," my mother said snidely.

"I rather enjoy it," I assured her.

"And no disrespect to my sister but her kitchen repertoire can get a bit repetitive, while Victor's cooking shows a lot of imagination. Since he moved to Greece he's totally sold me on vegetables," Barry said.

Leaving Barry and Violet Burke to bicker over whom got the first shower I grabbed a Lidl carrier bag and headed into the garden to have words with Guzim before he scooted off on his moped to his labouring job on the coast. The Albanian shed dweller was pegging assorted items of distinctly sad underclothing on a plastic washing line he had strung between a fence post and one of my orange trees. I reflected that Marigold would not be impressed by this arrangement since she would be forced to duck to avoid a slap in the face from Guzim's rather holey damp underpants or his grey tinged vest, said underwear looking as though it had not so much been laundered as treated to a quick rinse under the hosepipe. I recalled that on my one visit inside his shed his laundry had been strung up, dripping over his bed. I wondered if he had some ulterior motive for hanging it in my garden.

Swallowing my suspicion that the display of pathetic undies was a deliberate ploy to guilt me into donating my own pristine Y-fronts to the Albanian, I offered Guzim the carrier bag to encourage him to clean up the chicken droppings.

"*Argotera, tora einai ora ya douleia,*" he said with a broad toothless grin, promising to do it later, now it was time for work.

Before I had chance to remonstrate that he was slacking in his muck removal responsibilities, a responsibility he had volunteered for and profited from, Violet Burke appeared by my side. Still sporting the candlewick dressing gown and rollers, my mother wasted no time laying into Guzim, shouting that he was a disgusting specimen of manhood and he'd better think again if he thought his flashing antics would impress her.

Visibly flinching, his former grin replaced with a hangdog expression, Guzim squeaked "*Ti?*" He was completely clueless how he had managed to rile up this formidable woman who was clearly giving him a piece of her mind in a language he was unable to decipher.

Since the smell of chicken droppings really was quite ripe and likely to put my houseguests off spending time in the garden, I shamelessly decided to take advantage of Guzim's ignorance of my mother's tongue.

"*I mitera mou den mou aresei i myrodia tou muck, tha to kanei arrosto.*" Rather than translating Violet Burke's tirade I simply improvised, forgoing all mention of flashers and telling Guzim my mother hated the smell of muck and it would likely make her ill unless he cleaned it up.

"*Sygnomi Kyria.*" Guzim whimpered an apology to my mother, practically snatching the previously rejected carrier bag from my hand. Prostrating himself on the ground he began to scoop handfuls of chicken manure into the bag.

"I can see that I've got my work cut out for me this morning," my mother said once Guzim made his escape on the moped, the carrier bag of droppings dangling from the handlebars.

"There's no need for you to work, you're on holiday. I thought we could all enjoy a nice walk around the village," I said.

"I'm not walking anywhere with these swollen feet," my mother argued, pointing down to the roll of flab protruding from her flat lace-up shoes. "I'll stop here and give this hen house of yours a good disinfecting. My grandson was telling me he fancies a spot of sunbathing in the garden and I can't expect him to put up with this stink."

"The pong is a tad ripe," I agreed. Whilst Guzim certainly did an excellent job of caring for the chickens his attitude to actual hen house hygiene was definitely slapdash. Since Violet Burke seemed so set on cleaning things up I presumed she must have experience of raising poultry. Her current living arrangements over the chippy no doubt precluded her from keeping chickens now, perhaps a lifestyle choice she had once enjoyed. I certainly knew from my limited experience how satisfying it could be to raise an egg-laying brood.

"Do you miss keeping chickens?" I asked.

"Keeping chickens, I've never kept chickens. What put that daft idea in your head?"

"Oh, I just assumed you must have done, I wouldn't expect someone with no experience of fowls to voluntarily enter the chicken coop."

"I shouldn't think there's much difference between a mucky dwelling, whether it houses a bunch of smelly birds or human slobs. There's nothing that can't be tackled with some bleach, Vim, and good honest elbow grease."

"I wouldn't recommend venturing into the hen house if you're not used to the creatures, they can be a tad temperamental. I got a nasty swipe from the cockerel's spurs, it drew blood," I warned.

"Don't be so soft Victor, you just have to show them who's the boss. You don't half have some funny notions though. I'd like to know where you thought I kept chickens. Before I moved over the chippy I was in a two-up two-down terrace, I suppose you thought I kept a stash of livestock in the outside lavvy. Still I have to say you've got your garden nice here; it will be pleasant to put my feet up outdoors once

I've got rid of this pong."

"It's a shame that your feet aren't up to a walk around the village, I know Benjamin and Adam are looking forward to it. After our walk I will make a nice lunch for everyone."

"You could start by throwing that chicken in the oven," Violet Burke suggested, pointing at Raki. "It's a got a gammy leg, look. There's no point in coddling a deformed chicken Victor, best to put it out of its misery. It would make a lovely roast with all the trimmings."

"Raki's leg may have a slight abnormality but it doesn't impede her in anyway, she's an excellent layer."

"If you're too squeamish to wring its neck you only had to say, I don't mind giving it a go..."

"There will be no chicken murdering on my watch, I would rather turn vegetarian than willingly slaughter one of my flock," I protested. "How would you like it if I suggested you should be put on the scrap heap just because your feet are all bloated?"

"All right, keep your hair on, how was I to know I'd birthed one of them animal right's activists," she scoffed. "I wouldn't have suggested cooking it if I'd known you were such an animal lover."

"Since they can't speak for themselves I am happy to speak in defence of dumb animals," I said, realising I sounded a tad sanctimonious. Crossing my fingers behind my back I hoped that Marigold didn't expose my hypocrisy by revealing how eager I'd been to rid the house of superfluous kittens.

"I take it you don't object to me doing us all a nice bit of brekkie with these or does that count as murder by boiling?" my mother asked, sweeping up the basket of eggs Guzim had collected.

"Will you do them with soldiers?" I asked eagerly, choosing to ignore her obvious sarcasm.

Chapter 6

The Honey Man

G ranny's definitely got the touch when it comes to soft boiled eggs and soldiers," Benjamin said. He had really enjoyed having his new found Granny pampering him over the breakfast table, keeping his eggs piping hot in knitted egg cosies she had carted over from England. He had practically squealed in delight when she deftly topped his eggs, wielding the knife with as much skill as a guillotiner.

"Well the credit should really go to your father, he's the one who was so set on keeping chickens," Marigold pointed out.

"You can't beat a newly laid egg," I said proudly.

"You can if you scramble them," Adam guffawed.

The four of us were enjoying a morning stroll through the village, taking advantage of the relative coolness before the humidity set in. Since it was Adam's first time in Meli he was keen to explore the local area. Turning off the main street we started up a dirt path with a sharp incline, attracted by the distant sound of bells. After climbing in silence for fifteen minutes we paused to watch a collection of goats, the source of the melodic tinkling of bells, grazing in an olive grove adjacent to the path.

"They really are quite attractive specimens," Benjamin observed.

"I put my foot down when your father fancied getting a goat," Marigold said.

"Don't worry darling, I've gone off the idea completely. It seemed like a good plan when the garden was a weed infested wilderness, less so with all the vegetables and flowers we've cultivated. It's such a pity you boys missed out on our strawberry crop…"

"But the figs are just beginning to ripen," Marigold interrupted.

"I shall poach some figs in a dash of red wine and serve them with Greek yoghurt and honey for a light dessert this lunchtime," I said.

"That sounds glorious," Adam said approvingly.

"And if we have an excess of figs this year I will experiment with fig chutney," I said. Marigold had bottled some fig chutney the previous year, but I fancied livening up the recipe with a dash of port.

"You and your chutney, there's no need to get carried away," Marigold groaned, reminding me that we'd only just got rid of the last of the courgette chutney by palming it off on Dimitris' pig, even though such largesse technically flouted my dogged reservations about feeding swill to livestock.

The four of us stood aside at the sound of a motorbike approaching, waving in greeting as Giannis rode up. Giannis is a local fellow who only recently relocated to Meli from the big city. Apparently sick of soulless slick city living, he was homesick for his birth village and keen to carve a living from the great outdoors where he could feel at one with nature. From what I could gather Giannis had moved back in with his mother, taking charge of the family olives whilst starting a side-line in honey production and dabbling in motorcycle repairs. Giannis certainly stands out amidst the local population, not because he is notably tall, dark, handsome and muscular, which he certainly is, but rather because most of the population is pensioned off and Giannis is only just nearing thirty.

Giannis puts in the odd appearance in the taverna to be sociable, but the more than occasional late night roar of his motorcycle suggests he seeks his fun on the coast. I would hazard a guess that he's a bit of a babe magnet amongst the tourist women who remain blissfully unaware that the local Adonis now lives with his doting mother. Although such an arrangement is normal in these parts it may contradict the impression of muscular masculinity if independent foreign women realise he still allows his mother to mollycoddle him.

Drawing level with us Giannis cut the engine, removing his helmet as he dismounted and running his hands through his unruly black curls. "*Xreiazesai voitheia? Echete provlima me to aftokinito?*" Giannis said, offering help if we needed it and asking if we had a problem with the car.

"*Ochi efcharisto. Kanoun mia volta*," I replied, 'no thank you, we are talking a walk.' I was growing accustomed to locals offering assistance if they spotted us out walking, presuming the car must have broken down. It was practically unheard of for our Greek neighbours to walk for pleasure. Though we would often run into the local ladies in the olive groves, they were there with a purpose, collecting *horta*, the wild greens that are delicious when boiled and served with a squeeze of fresh lemon.

"Actually I think you got your Greek mixed up, you should have said *kanoume*, we are, you just told Giannis 'they' are walking," Marigold interrupted pedantically whilst Giannis' head swivelled back and forth between us. Since his English was non-existent he probably wondered what we were quibbling about. This was hardly the time for Marigold to start nit-picking over my grammar. Ignoring my wife and disregarding my hurt pride I asked Giannis what brought him up this way: "*Ti sas fernei edo?*"

"*Ta koutia melissas*," Giannis replied, saying that he was here for the bee boxes. My curiosity was sparked as I was interested to learn more about local honey production. Giannis then launched into a lengthy and no doubt informative diatribe about honey, barely pausing to take breath; at least I presume it would have been informative if I'd been able to understand his fast paced patter in an accent that bore little resemblance to the local dialect. He had clearly picked up some strange inflections whilst living in the big city.

I nodded along as though comprehending when I was able to pick out occasional words I was familiar with, such as *lofos* hill, *faskomilo* sage, and *thymari* thyme. Despite Marigold having publically corrected my grammar I noted her expression was one of blank fixation; she clearly didn't have a clue what Giannis was spouting on about either.

"*Ekpliktikos*," I said authoritatively when Giannis paused for breath, crossing my fingers that he had actually been talking about honey production. My response of 'wonderful' might cause offence if he'd actually been blathering on about some sickly scourge afflicting his bee colony. I made a mental note to carve out some time with my Greek text books and swat up on the relevant words relating to bee husbandry; it wouldn't do be caught out so unprepared the next time I ran into the local budding apiarist.

Remounting his motorbike Giannis bid us good day, leaving us with the parting words "*se des sto gamo*."

"Did the honey man just say he'd see us at the wedding?" Marigold asked.

"I think he did. How many people has Barry invited? I didn't even know he knew Giannis."

"Perhaps Cynthia extended an invitation, he'd definitely add a dishy touch to the wedding photographs," Marigold suggested. "You'd better have a word with Nikos and Dina. We need to make sure they prepare enough canapés to feed any random Greeks that turn up unexpectedly."

Giannis had only motorcycled to the next olive grove over. We watched with interest as he tended to the colourful bee boxes harbouring his colonies and I explained to the boys that the local honey he produced would be infused with the flavours of the local wild herbs.

"It's certainly getting awfully hot up here," Adam said, desperately looking around for shade. His words were our cue to make our way back to the village; the boys were not yet accustomed to the high temperature and it wouldn't do for them to come down with a nasty dose of sunstroke. Reaching the village I suggested a detour to the local shop, needing to pick up some Feta for lunch. Fortunately the plane trees lining the village square offered shade from the sun.

Marigold and I tentatively poked our heads in the shop before venturing inside, needing to steel ourselves in advance if the despicable Despina was serving behind the counter. To our great relief there was no sign of the wart faced harridan. The shop appeared busier than it had been lately, loyal customers apparently returning. We weren't sure if they had chosen to shop there again in order to gloat at Despina or if it was because the cantankerous woman had been relegated to the storeroom where she wouldn't be able to stir up malicious marital rumours or insult the customers.

We were greeted with a pleasant smile by her daughter Tina. Unsure of the accepted protocol when it came to bringing up the subject of close relatives being arrested, I decided it would be prudently tactful to keep schtum on the matter. However it appeared that Tina was positively eager to bring up the subject, announcing in the faltering English she liked to practice on us that her mother had returned to her own village for a break following the humiliation of her public arrest. Tina emphasised that normal service with a sunny disposition would resume, seemingly relieved that her mother wouldn't be there to scare off any remaining customers. Whilst Tina cut a prime *feta* of Feta cheese for the lunchtime dish I was planning, Marigold hissed at me that she was certain Tina had been the one to dob her mother in for illegal Sunday trading in order to entice the customers back.

I was happy that Despina's absence meant we could shop without running the risk of being cut down by her viperous tongue, whilst the boys filled their basket to overflowing with tempting uniquely Greek products.

Chapter 7

A Rather Constipated Lunch

A fter putting the shopping away the four of us headed straight down to the garden, surprised to find no sign of my mother. Marigold and Adam sank back in a couple of sun loungers with a pitcher of chilled orange juice, whilst Benjamin joined me in a wander round the garden. We breathed in the delicious scent of Marigold's herb garden, admired her beautiful display of flowering plants blooming in earthenware pots, and marvelled at the delicacy of the deep pink bougainvillea trained to grow against the wall of the stone staircase. Benjamin was suitably impressed with the healthy appearance of the vegetables, amazed when I described their astonishing growth spurts.

Naturally I shared the credit for the vegetables with Guzim: it was hard to forget his contribution when his holey underpants whacked Benjamin in the face, but at least they had dried in the sunshine. I made a mental note to broach with Guzim the delicate subject of finding a more discreet spot to hang his washing that didn't involve his pants flapping about in my garden. If he proved stubborn I wasn't above bribing him with a new and unopened packet of my own Marks and Spencer Y-fronts if it would spare our guests the intrusive sight of his smalls.

"The chickens are looking healthy," Benjamin observed as we stood by the wire netting enclosing the chicken run, watching the flock pecking away in search of grubs. The strong smell of disinfectant emanating from the chicken's domain worried me a tad; I hoped that Violet Burke hadn't concocted some evil scheme to murder my brood by dousing the ground with poisonous quantities of bleach. I reflected that if she had indeed harboured such a plan in order to facilitate her desire for a roast dinner with all the trimmings, it would be in vain. A chicken would come down with sodium hypochlorite poisoning if it ingested enough of a lethal dose of bleach to see it off, thus making it unfit for human consumption.

"I had to pull out the old 'thinking of going veggie card' to dissuade my mother from throwing one of the chickens in the oven," I told Benjamin. "She had her eye on Raki because of its gammy leg. Fancy her thinking I'd be willing to eat one of my brood."

"Oh dear, Granny can be a bit blunt. Still you have to admit Dad that when you first thought of keeping chickens I bet you didn't expect to come to regard them as pets."

"That's a fair point, they have rather grown on me," I admitted. "I think it came from watching their individual personality traits develop. I was rather taken aback to discover how intelligent they are."

"Well as long as you don't go overboard and get too attached. I was reading the most ridiculous piece in the paper the other day about some woman in the States who was shelling out a small fortune to have a prosthetic leg fixed to one of her chickens…or perhaps it was a duck?"

"That is definitely going way over the top," I laughed. Fond though I was of the chickens I had no intention of forking over some ludicrous sum to the veterinarian surgeon. Fortunately the afflicted chicken managed to hop along perfectly well on its gammy leg without the assistance of an artificial limb.

"Speaking of Granny, I wonder where she has got to," Benjamin said.

"Well she was adamant that she was staying here to clean out the chicken coop," I said.

"You don't suppose she headed into the hen house and passed out in the heat?" Benjamin suggested. Although it struck me as unlikely I agreed we ought to check just to be on the safe side. I imagined we'd never hear the end of it if the cockerel was pecking and swiping at a cornered and cowering Violet Burke, and we failed to come to her rescue. Whilst it didn't strike me as a likely scenario she had admitted to no actual experience of chickens and the cockerel did have a vindictive streak.

The hen house proved to be empty of both chickens and humans. It was clear that Violet Burke had been inside as the place practically sparkled with cleanliness, the wooden planks bearing testament to a thorough buffing with furniture polish, all traces of the stench of chickens eradicated.

"What's that smell?" Benjamin asked, sniffing inquisitively. "I can't quite put my finger on it but I think there are accents of vanilla."

Inhaling deeply the strong smell of bleach assaulted my naval passages, but I had to agree there were definite undertones of vanilla.

"Perhaps she gave it a blast with a can of air freshener," I suggested.

"Hold on, isn't that Mum's fancy scented candle?"

Sighing in exasperation I snuffed out the wick. Surely Violet Burke had the sense to realise the fire hazard a burning candle presented in a wooden construction filled with straw. I would need to sneak the decorative candle back into the grand salon before Marigold realised it was missing.

I was rather taken aback to notice that a couple of Marigold's best cushions had replaced the usual straw bedding; perhaps my mother was going soft in the head. Relieved that we didn't need to rescue Violet Burke from the clutches of the vicious cockerel, we stepped outside, happy to escape the discordant smells of bleach and vanilla.

Benjamin and I exchanged puzzled glances as the sound of my mother's voice pervaded the garden; it appeared to be drifting over from next door. With as much discretion as I could muster I peered over the garden wall, hoping Kyria Maria didn't spot me and accuse me of being a peeping Tom. I was surprised to discover Violet Burke sitting on a hard backed kitchen chair in the neighbouring garden, deep in conversation with Maria.

It was an amusing spectacle to say the least since both elderly women were talking away at each other, nineteen to the dozen in their respective languages. They clearly had no interest at all in what the other had to say, probably just as well since they were both clueless to what the other was actually saying. The odd scene certainly supported the old adage of being in love with the sound of one's own voice. In spite of my best efforts to be discreet Kyria Maria clocked my presence, acknowledging me with a cheery wave.

"Are, there you are Victor, give me a hand back over this wall," my mother instructed.

"What were you doing next door Granny?" Benjamin asked as we hauled her bulbous frame.

"I was just having a nice cuppa with Maria. Well I say nice but she's got a funny idea of what makes a decent cuppa. It was as weak as dishwater and I could swear there were bits of twigs floating round in the cup," my mother complained. "I'll have to get some proper PG Tips inside her when she comes round here for a brew."

"But how do you understand each other?" Benjamin asked, an expression of genuine confusion plastered on his face.

"I think we're both a bit past all that soul seeking bonding you young ones are into, sometimes it's just nice to have a bit of company over a cup of tea," Violet Burke said realistically. "Ooh, my feet aren't half giving me some gip, I think I'll just pop upstairs and give them a good soaking in the washing up bowl before lunch. How you survive without a bath tub I'll never know."

"Remind me to invest in a new plastic bowl later," I said to my son, trying to get my head around the contradictory notion of a woman seemingly obsessed with hygiene paying such scant regard to the necessity of retaining a sterile receptacle for cleaning dishes in.

"Right, let's get started on picking something

tasty for lunch. I think a simple fresh salad will go well with the cheese dish I plan to whip up. Grab some tomatoes Ben."

"Straight from the vine, cushty as Del Boy would say."

"I don't suppose he came across a lot of tomatoes on the vine in Peckham," I quipped.

After selecting lettuce, cucumbers, tomatoes and green peppers for the salad, we moved onto the fig tree. "Wow I had no idea figs were so black," Benjamin exclaimed.

"They're not black. They have more of a purplish hue I'd say."

"Well this one is as black as night," Benjamin contradicted, reaching out to pluck the fig that had grabbed his attention.

"Well I've never come across an actual black one…"

"Oh gross, it's alive," Benjamin shouted, yanking his hand away from the chosen fruit and shaking it wildly to dislodge something presumably nasty. Peering at the now rejected fig I realised it was actually being devoured in front of our very eyes; what Ben had presumed to be shiny black skin was in reality a mass of writhing black ants sucking the life from the fruit. In seconds the fig was no more.

"Quick, grab some ant free figs before they move onto their next target," I cried. It appeared there was a very fine line between allowing fresh figs to ripen on the branches and the risk of having them over ripen, only to be completely annihilated by rapacious insects. I made a mental note to gather the figs before they fully ripened in future. "Best if you don't mention the ants to your mum, she still gets squeamish if she's reminded of the time some got trapped in her bra."

"What are you doing with that?" Violet Burke asked, watching me dip pieces of Feta cheese in beaten egg, flour and sesame seeds.

"I'm hoping to replicate a rather tasty dish of Feta with sesame seeds and honey that we had in town. It was actually wrapped in filo pastry, but alas pastry isn't my forte so I thought I'd omit the filo and pan fry it instead."

"Decent pastry needs lard, my lad. I could have shown you how we do proper pastry in Lancashire if my lard hadn't been confiscated at the airport. I bet those interfering customs officials have knocked up some lovely homemade pies out of my lard."

"Warrington's in Cheshire, not Lancashire,"

I pointed out, trying to dislodge images of stodgy lard from my brain.

"That's as maybe since they messed with it, but when I was a lass it was still in Lancashire. I can't say I've much appetite for eating seeds, it's all a bit hippy-like for me."

"I acquired quite a taste for them when I taste tested bird feed…" Marigold confided.

"You what?" Violet Burke interrupted, staring at Marigold as though she had lost her mind.

"Back in England Marigold was a pet food taster," I explained.

"There's a lovely mix of seeds in the best brands of bird food," Marigold said. "Safflower, sunflower and sorghum, and of course sesame, make for a lovely blend."

Looking Marigold up and down Violet Burke decreed "It's no wonder you're so thin if you think birdseed passes for food."

Practically preening in pleasure at what she presumed was a compliment on her trim figure, Marigold waltzed off to the bathroom.

"I never heard the like," Violet Burke blurted, "paying someone to taste test bird food. Suet, now that's a proper diet for birds. That wife of yours could do with feeding up on suet to put some meat on her bones."

"Marigold has a lovely figure." Even though Marigold was out of earshot I felt it was my husbandly duty to defend her, thinking at least she didn't have a spare roll of flab resembling said suet bulging out of her shoes.

Marigold returned to the kitchen, rolling her eyes in exasperation when my mother said "Happen I'll throw a Fray Bentos in the oven, I can't say I fancy foreign cheese dipped in bird food."

"Just try it Mother, please," I urged.

"Well if it will make you happy I'll give it a go, but I've a feeling it will end up inside those chickens of yours."

"Victor has a strict policy of not serving any leftovers to the chickens, he can get a bit anal about cross contamination," Marigold said, whipping up an olive oil and balsamic dressing for the salad. "He's got a bee in his bonnet about foot and mouth."

Marigold's casual reference to bonnets made me wince; I expected my wife to be more sensitive to my feelings. I glanced surreptitiously at Violet Burke, concerned she may be overcome with painful memories triggered by the bonnet reference. It appeared to have gone over her head; she was completely engrossed in examining her feet, now residing in my washing up bowl.

"You may well sneer at my concerns but feeding scraps to poultry has been illegal since 2001," I reminded Marigold.

"I'm sure the prisons are full to bursting with criminal types caught feeding scraps to their chickens," she retorted. I couldn't help but notice my wife and my mother exchanging bemused eye rolls; it appeared they were finally bonding, albeit it at my expense.

"It seems that whilst you aren't particularly fussy what the chickens eat you do seem overly concerned that they have comfortable beds," I said to my mother.

Responding to Marigold's raising of a questioning eyebrow, I elaborated, telling her that Violet Burke had appropriated her best cushions for the hen house.

"There could be anything breeding in that stinking straw mess, you can't throw straw in the washing machine and kill off any nasties in the boil wash cycle," Violet Burke insisted. "You can't expect me to eat eggs that have been sitting around in flea infested straw, there's something to be said for cardboard egg boxes."

"Those cushions were looking a bit tired, it's

a good excuse for a shopping trip. It's just a good job they aren't stuffed with feathers, it may be a bit cannibalistic for the chickens," Marigold said, surprising me by the ease in which she sided with Violet Burke. My mind boggled at Marigold's thought process; she seemed to be under the impression that my chickens were so starved that they would be reduced to eating their own bedding.

"This Feta wouldn't look out of place in one of my stylised shoots," Benjamin said, admiring the way the drizzle of warm honey added a golden tinge to my cheese masterpiece as the five of us sat down to lunch.

"It's not too bad, but it would definitely be improved with a dollop of mushy peas," my mother pronounced.

"But we have fresh salad from the garden," I pointed out.

"I'll give it a miss. It's not that I'm averse to a bit of cucumber and lettuce, but Marigold's gone and ruined it by drowning it in oil."

"Vi, the extra virgin olive oil complements the salad perfectly, it is how salad is always served in Greece," Marigold said.

"Happen they started the habit because the

nation was constipated," my mother mused. "I remember when they sold little bottles of olive oil in the chemists to use as a laxative…"

"Surely that was cod liver oil," Benjamin interrupted.

"I thought it was castor oil," Adam said.

"I think it was syrup of figs that was sold as a laxative," Marigold piped up. "Chemists used to sell olive oil for earwax and cod liver oil was a supplement, ghastly stuff."

"I remember being threatened with a spoonful of cod liver oil if I didn't eat my greens," I recalled with a shudder. "It really was vile."

"Olive oil is becoming very popular in England now Granny, it's acclaimed for its health giving properties," Benjamin assured her.

"Well my bowels are regular enough without it, thanks all the same."

"I really don't think the state of your bowels is a suitable topic of conversation while we're eating," Marigold objected.

"Well oily salad is not to my taste, you can't beat a nice dollop of Heinz salad cream. Never mind, I'll fill up on pudding. What are we having Victor?" my mother said.

"I've poached some fresh figs in red wine

and star anise. I will serve them with Greek yoghurt and honey."

My mother's face a picture of disgust, she blurted "You've got laxatives on the brain, first oil and now figs."

"Surely you're thinking of prunes Granny," Benjamin interjected.

"Anyway if you insist on feeding us figs I think they'll go better with tinned custard," my mother continued. "I quite like to dip my fig rolls in custard for a bit of a treat."

"These are fresh figs Granny, have you ever tried them?" Benjamin asked.

"You daft lad, where exactly would I be getting fresh figs in Warrington? I don't go along with all this fancy imported fruit, I like to know my fruit has been grown local, not messed about with in foreign parts. You can't beat a good British apple, pear or banana."

Adam and Benjamin almost choked on their Feta when Violet Burke insisted she enjoyed a nice banana grown in Warrington. Ignoring the boys I attempted to reason with my mother, saying, "But that's the whole point, we also enjoy eating fresh locally grown products rather than imported ones. It's just that our local produce is different to what we were used to back in England."

"And you can't get more local than Dad's garden," Benjamin added, having finally controlled his mirth.

"Take asparagus," I said. "We have a bountiful supply of wild asparagus growing locally whilst the imported stuff is a shocking price up in *Alfa Beta*."

"I love a nice bit of asparagus, but the stuff that grows here is woody and fibrous," Marigold said. "I know that you're quite keen on it Victor, but personally I find it inedible unless it's hidden in a quiche."

"Mum, the asparagus you enjoyed in England was imported from Spain so it rather undermines the point we're making about eating locally grown," Benjamin said.

"How come you've got a cupboard full of Fray Bentos then if you don't eat imported?" my mother demanded.

Catastrophe chose that moment to jump onto my lap. Swooshing her shortened tail in my face she created a distraction, sparing me from answering my mother. I reflected that the cat had its uses after all and I would probably get more sense from it than I would from my wife and mother.

Chapter 8

A Suspicious Corridor Lurker

The hospital lobby was eerily quiet when Barry and I arrived mid-afternoon to visit Litsa. The locals had warned us to expect nothing short of a scrum if we turned up at the *nosokomeio* during the morning when the arrivals area would be heaving with impatient Greeks and their myriad relatives, clutching tickets and congregating outside the doors of various specialists, but by siesta time the place resembled a morgue. I had assumed that we would simply enquire at the reception desk for directions to Litsa's room, but there was no one manning the desk to question. Decidedly out of our depth we wandered through the silent lobby, the Greek lettering on the signs for various departments confusing us, the only recognisable sign being the pictorial one for the toilets.

"Ah, I can see how it works, look we have to follow one of these coloured lines," Barry announced. "But which one?"

"I would hazard a guess that the red one leads to accident and emergency. Let me flip through the dictionary and see if I can make any sense of these signs," I said, having sensibly taken the precaution of bringing along my Greek to English dictionary, in addition to the pocket English to Greek one I was in the habit of carting along everywhere. Locating the Greek letters in the correct order in the dictionary proved to be a painstakingly slow process since I still found the Euclidean alphabet a tad confusing, having a tendency to discombobulate my *omega* with my *omicron*, and my *epsilon* with my *upsilon*.

"Well we definitely don't want to follow that sign, it leads to gynaecology."

I was spared the long and arduous task of

translating each sign when a woman clad in a pristine white uniform and crocs appeared in the lobby. Sighing in relief at the sight of a medical professional I approached her, asking in Greek where we would find Litsa's room number.

"Tell me in English," the woman replied, making me wonder what gave me away as a foreigner or if I had mispronounced a Greek word. As we followed her directions up two flights of stairs and along various corridors I asked Barry what he thought gave me away as a non-Greek.

"I expect it's the socks and sandals," he said.

"I didn't think they were so obvious paired with long trousers," I replied, having deliberately rejected even well pressed shorts as unsuitable for hospital visiting.

"Also your skin is a bit soft looking; Greeks of your age tend to look a bit more weather-beaten," Barry said. He had a point, his own complexion was already more rugged than mine after a few weeks of manual labour in the sun.

"Well I have no intention of giving up my high factor sun screen, without adequate protection I would stand out like a spit-roasted tourist."

We exhaled in relief when we finally located the department giving bed room to Litsa, creeping silently down the corridor until we located the correct room number. Peering through the open door we surveyed four beds, only three of them occupied.

We immediately spotted Litsa sitting up in a bed next to the window, a look of pain etched on her wrinkled features. Her brother Matthias and a woman we guessed was the niece from Athens were dozing in chairs by the bed. As we entered the room Litsa turned towards us, a smile of delight giving her weatherworn creases an instant face-lift, the turn of her head revealing a nasty black eye and a badly bruised cheek.

Holding her hands out in welcome, Litsa gushed, "*Barry mou, eiste toso kalo agori yia na erthei,*" saying he was such a good boy to come and visit her. As Barry bent down, leaning in to offer a hug, the   niece stirred enough to let out a warning cry, "*Proseche, einai ponous na pesei kato.*"

Barry turned to me, gesturing he didn't understand.

"You need to be careful, Litsa is in pain from falling down," I translated.

Despite her obvious discomfort Litsa rallied

enough to insist, *"Ela Barry mou, dose mou ena fil-aki,"* telling him to come and give her a kiss. Finally noticing that Barry was not alone, Litsa greeted me with a feeble wave, not bothering to extend an invitation to kiss her. Whilst clearly appreciating that I had made the effort to visit, it was Barry who she doted on and who was the centre of her attention. Keeping hold of Barry's hand she introduced him to her niece Agathe, telling her that Barry was such a good boy, so kind and thoughtful. Barry's blushes suggested he understood what Litsa was saying when the old woman told her niece that he was getting married that week, but if she was thirty years younger she would have snapped him up as he would have made her a lovely husband.

Insisting I take her seat, Agathe jumped up, plumping Litsa's pillows and brushing an invisible speck from her nightie. Her movements woke Matthias who shook his head as he stirred, surprised to see Barry and me by his sister's bedside. Having been there since dawn he looked bone weary, relieved to follow Agathe's bidding to clear off and get himself a coffee.

Attempting to disguise her own tiredness Agathe admitted she had spent the previous night in the chair by the bed and would do the same again later. She was hopeful that Litsa could go home the next day if the doctor was satisfied with her progress; Litsa had been very lucky to suffer nothing more than nasty bruising, tests revealing that the knock to her head had not resulted in any neurological complications.

I assured Agathe that we would sit with her aunt if she wanted to go and freshen up and get a coffee. She appeared initially reluctant to abandon her aged relative to two foreign strangers until Litsa shooed her out, saying *"oi Angloi tha menoun mazi mou, Barry kai Victor einai toso kala agoria."* I was touched that Litsa acknowledged me when she told Agathe the English men would stay with her; we were both such good boys.

Litsa told us that she had fallen over stepping out of the house, banging her head against the wall as she tried to steady herself. Not familiar with all the words she used I nevertheless think that she joked that she would have to borrow Cynthia's bridal veil to cover up her bruises for the wedding; at least I hoped she was joking as I couldn't see Cynthia willingly handing it over. After a few minutes of small talk Litsa's eyes closed and we sat quietly whilst she dozed, careful not to disturb the other two occupants of the room.

Loud snoring from the bed opposite Litsa's indicated its occupant was sleeping, whilst a frail old woman with almost translucent skin in the bed adjacent to Litsa's was silently rigid, only an occasional strangulated snort belying the impression she was a corpse. Surprisingly neither patient had the compulsory quota of relatives in attendance. With nothing to do I stood up to take in the view from the window, noting it overlooked a square courtyard surrounded by another three walls lined with identical windows. I presumed that the throng of pigeons perching on windowsills were the reason the windows remained closed despite the heat; it would be an unhygienic nightmare if the flying vermin gained access to the hospital rooms.

A sudden flurry of activity heralded the arrival of a new admittance destined for the fourth bed. A well-dressed woman started barking orders at the two teenage girls accompanying her; responding to her commands they began unpacking a travel bag, passing her bottles of cleaning products and cloths. She immediately began spraying every already pristine surface, wiping everything down vigorously. I doubt a single germ could have survived her meticulous scouring. Their arrival was followed by an orderly pushing a woman in a wheelchair who was helped into the fourth bed. After subjecting the plastic hospital chairs to a rigorous scrub down the woman finally sat down and greeted us. *"Eisai Geramanos?"*

I was familiar with the question 'are you German' since many of the ancient hitchhikers I picked up on the mountain road asked the same thing before settling into the Punto. I found they tended to relax and feel at ease in my presence when I responded that I was English. The woman immediately began chatting to us in painfully stilted English, telling us her mother had just been wheeled in from a different ward, and that she and her sister were taking it in turns to spend the night by their mother's bedside. Expressing her opinion that it was shocking how the families of the other two patients were neglecting their relatives, she jumped up to spray clean their bedside tables and their bed rails just in case they had anything contagious that was capable of bed hopping. Sensing that she was itching to wipe down the area around Litsa's bed, I gave her the go-ahead, doubting that Litsa would object since Barry reported she kept a scrupulously clean home.

Nudging me with his elbow Barry nodded towards the open door, leaning in to whisper "that's the third time that chap has paused for a good look in. I wonder what his game is."

Looking over I saw a shabbily dressed man in his forties lurking suspiciously in the doorway.

"Perhaps he's trying to locate a relative," I suggested.

"Or he could be a pervert stalking the corridors to eye up helpless women," Barry hissed.

"Or a thief with his eye out for valuables," I added, sending a stern look in the lurker's direction. As the man scurried away Barry moved to the doorway, reporting back that he wasn't lingering outside other rooms. I was glad that Litsa had the two of us there to protect her from prowling strangers with potentially nefarious intentions.

"He could be look for the empty bed," the well-dressed woman interjected. "My sister to tell me the last night she help my mother in the bathroom to pluck the hair from the chin. When they come back a stranger woman was the sleep in my mother's bed."

"Surely not," I gasped.

"*Einai alitheia*." After confirming it was true the woman continued, "My sister wake the woman and she say she the wife of the man with the cataracts across the corridor, she so uncomfortable in the chair she see the empty bed and climb in. My sister so the angry, she must to change the sheet and to clean the everything again."

I exchanged a bemused glance with Barry at this ridiculous tale. Before we had chance to comment the woman enlightened us that the healthy bed hopper could have had a good night's sleep by simply hiring a comfortable lounge chair to sleep in if she objected to spending the night sitting upright on plastic.

Barry nudged me sharply in the ribs again, alerting me to the return of the corridor lurker, his eyes lingering over the four women in their beds in a decidedly shifty fashion. The well-dressed woman sprang from her seat, slamming the door in his face. With the door firmly closed the room became unbearably hot so I nonchalantly opened the window a tad, considering it was worth risking an influx of pigeons for a breath of fresh air. The well-dressed woman immediately objected, asking if I was trying to kill her mother off by letting the cold in, seemingly oblivious that the outside temperature was creeping towards forty degrees centigrade. Having been put firmly in my place I closed the window without uttering a word, hoping Agathe would soon return so that we could make our escape from the airless room.

We were taken completely by surprise when the door was flung open and Spiros put in an appearance, appearing equally taken aback to discover our presence. Rushing over to deposit kisses on our cheeks, Spiros seemed distracted. Complaining "How you to stand the hot in here?" Spiros immediately opened the window, earning a withering look from the well-dressed woman. I couldn't help but wonder if she had somehow crossed paths with Marigold.

"Spiro, we didn't expect to see you here," I said. "Are you visiting Litsa too?"

"No, I am the here on the funeral business, I get the call to come for the dead woman, but when I to get here I find out she still the patient in this room," Spiros shouted, his brow furled in anger.

Staring at the corpse like figure in the bed next to Litsa's, Spiros threw his hands up in a gesture of frustration, swearing *"to ilithio malaka,"* before stomping out to the corridor. Two minutes later Spiros returned, dragging the shifty corridor lurker by the collar and loudly berating him in angry Greek. The pair of them left the room as abruptly as they'd entered, the lurker looking even shiftier than he had earlier. I was clueless what Spiros had shouted at the lurker, but Barry was able to enlighten me since the builder's Greek he had been cramming up on apparently included some of Spiros' rather lurid expletives. I won't besmirch this tale by penning such vulgar words here, but the gist of what Barry repeated concerned Spiros swearing like a scalded navvy because the shifty chap hadn't waited until his grandmother was actually dead before calling out the undertaker.

Hoping to catch up with Spiros, I left Barry sitting with Litsa, promising to return with a couple of coffees. After making my way back through the quiet corridors I found Spiros perched on the wall outside the lobby entrance, gesturing wildly with a cigarette to an invisible audience as he chuntered away on his mobile. I wasn't accustomed to seeing the usual placid natured Spiros in a spat of temper.

"Can you to believe some the people?" Spiros asked me after disconnecting the call. "That fool to telephone me to bury the grandmother who not the dead. How you to say in English, the cheap roller…"

"Cheapskate," I corrected.

"Yes, the cheapskate, he think to get the discount before the rigor mortis set in. I am the professional Victor, this is the insult."

"It is outrageous," I sympathised. "It is certainly disgraceful behaviour to try to arrange someone's burial before they have passed."

"I talking with the hospital administrator on the phone, she the furious. She tell the security to throw from the hospital the grandson of the old woman and she come now to the hospital to find the other family of the old woman," Spiros said. "It is the time waste Victor. I had the plan to spend the afternoon to swim with the Sampaguita. I even to arrange the Kyria Kompogiannopoulou to look after the uncle."

"Well it's good that you've persuaded a local woman to share his care," I said.

"Yes, she is the willing to help now that the Sampaguita live with the uncle, she not to worry about the reputation."

"It may not be too late to still spend some quality time with Sampaguita. If you can persuade Kyria Kompopoulougian to look after your uncle this evening…"

"Kyria Kompogiannopoulou," Spiros corrected.

"Her name is a bit of a tongue twister," I admitted "but I was going to suggest that perhaps the two of you could join us for dinner at the coast. Marigold is driving our houseguests down in the Punto, I'm sure she'll be happy to bring Sampaguita along too."

Accepting the invitation with delight Spiros, took another call on his mobile. "*Erchomai tora*," he said to the caller, explaining to me the hospital administrator had arrived in her office and he must meet her at once. As he asked me to pass on his good wishes to Litsa, two burly security guards marched past us, physically escorting the suspicious corridor lurker from the premises.

Chapter 9

Avoiding the Stomach Pump

fter taking my leave from Spiros I recalled that I had promised Barry I
would return bearing coffee. As I set
about trying to locate the hospital canteen I
passed a male orderly precariously juggling
some take-away cups. Intercepting him I asked
directions, once again taken aback when he replied in English, telling me the canteen coffee
would kill me off and instead directing me to a
coffee shop opposite the hospital. Whilst reflecting I was certainly in the best place if I needed

my stomach pumping, I heeded his advice and headed outside again.

The slew of hospital employees queuing up for take-outs seemed to endorse the orderly's opinion that the coffee was a safer bet from this establishment. Waiting patiently for my turn I hoped that Agathe would have returned to her aunt's bedside by the time I got back with the drinks; the stuffy hospital room was a dismal place to while away such a lovely afternoon. My ears pricked up when I suddenly heard English being spoken, the man in front of me saying "How much? Sorry I don't understand."

Clearly the woman serving him didn't understand English, simply repeating in Greek "*pente kai miso.*"

After giving the fellow the discreet once over and noting his pallid complexion and casual garb, I made an educated guess that he was a holidaymaker out of his depth. Sensing the Englishman's embarrassment as he stared blankly at some coins in the palm of his hand, I stepped in to offer my assistance, telling him that his bill amounted to five and a half euros.

"Oh thanks very much," he said as I took the liberty of picking out the necessary coins. "I really wanted to get a couple of cups of tea but I couldn't make myself understood, so I just grabbed two bottles of water out of the fridge and pointed at a couple of pies in case my wife finds the hospital food inedible."

"Let me order that tea for you," I offered, placing his order along with my own request for two coffees.

"That's awfully good of you. I'm very impressed that you know the lingo."

Since everyone I had spoken to since arriving at the hospital had made a point of replying in English, I had once again begun to doubt my own competence in the Greek language. Whilst relieved that the woman behind the counter had taken the order I placed in Greek without looking at me as though I had two heads, I realised that it would not take much to impress an Englishman who had no grasp at all of the language and would be clueless that I frequently botched it with my mangled pronunciation.

"I live here in Greece," I told him as we waited for our drinks. "And your wife is a patient in the hospital?"

"Yes, unfortunately she came a cropper during a guided tour of Ancient Olympia last week. She tripped over and twisted her ankle quite badly, but she does hate to make a fuss. It was only last night when it ballooned up rather alarmingly that we realised it might be more serious than a sprain. The lady who runs our hotel insisted on driving us to the hospital and now Lynn is stuck in a bed here."

"How dreadful," I sympathised, immediately thanking my lucky stars that it hadn't happened on one of my tours. A badly turned ankle was a disaster waiting to happen considering how many tourists flouted the advice to wear sensible shoes, placing vanity above practicality and turning up in heels to traipse round the ruins.

"I'm Rodney by the way," he introduced himself.

"Victor, nice to meet you. I'll walk back over with you," I offered after helping him identify the necessary coins for the tea.

"It's all rather daunting having Lynn in a Greek hospital," Rodney confided as we made our way back through the labyrinth of hospital corridors. Our circuitous route carefully avoided the lifts since I was reluctant to breathe in hospital germs that may be defying hygiene standards and festering in such a confined space. "Have you got a family member here too?"

"No, my brother-in-law and I are visiting an elderly lady from our village. We're just giving her niece a breather since she pulled an all-nighter by her aunt's bedside."

"She spent the whole night by the hospital bed?" Rodney asked in surprise. "I couldn't make head or tail of the visiting hours."

"Yes, it's not the same as we're used to in England, they don't really have visiting hours as such. Over here it is expected that family members will stay with their hospitalised relatives, they are rather expected to do the things that nurses would do back in England," I explained.

"Oh no, I didn't realise, I'd never have gone off on the Vathia trip today if I'd known I was expected to stay with Lynn."

"You weren't to know, I'm sure it will be fine," I reassured him, thinking the staff may have found an Englishman who couldn't converse in their language a bit of a hindrance.

"Did you enjoy the trip to Vathia?" I asked as we took the stairs, presuming Rodney had joined Cynthia's tour.

"Actually it was a bit of a let-down. I'd rather been looking forward to it, but the guide was not only incompetent but completely disinterested, she didn't know anything about the history of the area."

I bristled on Cynthia's behalf at such a slight; after all she was about to become family. Cynthia may not be as well versed as me in the intricacies of historical details, but she is more than adequate in her role as guide.

"And I have to say her atrocious habit of adding the word like to every utterance rather grated on my nerves," Rodney added.

"A ghastly habit indeed," I agreed. Experiencing a light bulb moment I realised that for some reason Tiffany must have taken Cynthia's place as the tour guide on the Vathia excursion. "Now what room number is your wife in?"

Surprised to hear that Rodney's wife was in the same room as Litsa I made a mental list of the other three occupants, narrowing his wife down to the snorer. Approaching the room we passed the well-dressed woman and her teenage daughters. She informed me that they were just heading out to the nearest supermarket to stock up on more cleaning supplies.

Looking rather like a spare part, Barry was propping up the corridor outside Litsa's room. "The cleaner is inside," he explained.

"Have Agathe or Kostas returned yet?" I asked hopefully after introducing Barry to Rodney.

"You mean Matthias," Barry corrected. "Not a sight or sound of either of them. I hope they aren't taking liberties, but it doesn't feel right leaving Litsa alone before they get back."

"Well at least she doesn't need to worry about that shifty corridor lurker, Spiros arranged for security to escort him off the premises," I said. "By the way Rodney here was on the Vathia tour today, but it seems that Tiffany led it rather than Cynthia."

Raising a puzzled eyebrow Barry sighed, standing aside to make way for the cleaner to drag her mop bucket out of the room. "Perhaps last night's wine caught up with her, but she looked chirpy enough this morning."

Rodney's wife Lynn was now sitting up in bed. Rodney immediately began apologising to his wife, telling her he'd had no idea that it was the done thing to stay by her bedside day and night.

"Oh fiddles," Lynn said, brushing off his apology. "I've had a lovely sleep; you'd have been bored out of your brain sitting around here all day breathing in disinfectant and getting under everyone's feet. Oh is that a cup of tea? It's just what I fancied. I have to say everyone has been just marvellous. I couldn't have blamed them if they'd plastered up the wrong foot really, not with me not being able to speak Greek. I've picked up the word for foot though, it's *podi*. I think I'll pass on that pie dear, that lady's daughter told me the staff will be wheeling the meals in at any minute. Now tell me all about your day."

Lynn's attitude was certainly refreshing, remaining cheery and making the best of being confined to a hospital bed in a foreign country.

Litsa insisted that Barry and I leave, but since there was still no sign of Agathe and Matthias, Barry refused to desert the old lady. We had only just settled back into the chairs by the bed when the evening meal was delivered to the patients, even though it was still technically the afternoon. I surveyed the contents of the tray with interest, noting an appetiser of sliced cucumber and half a tomato, followed by a main course comprising a boiled chicken leg, a whole boiled courgette and a whole boiled carrot. It all looked rather cold, anaemic and unappetising. I made a mental note to tell Marigold that if I was ever confined to the hospital she should deliver a tasty takeaway from Nikos' taverna.

Despite my reservations about the food Lynn appeared delighted with the contents of her tray, exclaiming "oh this does look tasty, I do love Greek food. When poor Rodney was under the National Health with his piles can you believe they tried to serve him a rather sad salad with mashed potatoes on the side? They were obviously reconstituted from a packet, I'd be shocked if they'd been anywhere near an actual potato."

As Litsa struggled to cut the chicken with the plastic cutlery, Agathe finally returned. Speaking slowly and precisely for our benefit she apologised for being gone so long, explaining that Matthias had taken a funny turn in the canteen and had to be rushed through to accident and emergency. I was relieved that I could just about understand her Greek, pleased to recall the word for the emergency department which I'd come across in the dictionary earlier.

Barry and I exchanged anxious glances, worried that we were about to be roped in to play nursemaids for Matthias. It was one thing to visit his sister, but we barely knew Matthias, as evidenced by the fact that we'd been addressing him by the wrong name. I certainly didn't feel that a familiarity with his proclivity for eating raw garlic obligated us to clean out his bed pan or wipe the dribble from his chin.

"It may not be very neighbourly of us but I think we're going to have to play the 'we don't understand card' if they expect us to hang around and play nurse for Matthias," Barry hissed. "I'm a bit worried about Cynthia since you said she wasn't on the Vathia trip."

"Thank goodness for that," I exhaled in relief. "We're already going to be late meeting the others and Marigold will have kittens if I don't turn up soon to take Violet Burke off her hands. Let's try and sneak away sharpish."

Fortunately we didn't need to sneak anywhere because a doctor arrived who spoke excellent English and was happy to fill us in. He told us that Matthias had simply overdone it, but Agathe had hired a comfortable lounge chair for him to sleep in by Litsa's bedside rather than drive home. Litsa exclaimed in delight when the doctor assured her that she could go home the next day, promising us she'd be at the wedding.

It appeared we timed our departure just right, exiting the hospital room just as one of the pesky pigeons that had been hovering on the outside windowsill made a bold entrance in a flurry of wings. Giving Barry a brusque push I hissed, "Just pretend that you haven't noticed."

Chapter 10

Dining out on Weeds

A bout time too, my stomach thinks my throat's been cut," Violet Burke carped when Barry and I arrived thirty minutes late at the coastal taverna. I was rather taken aback that her complaint was somewhat softened by her teasing tone. Mindful of my mother's demands about not eating late as it would mess up her digestive constitution we had agreed to meet at the unheard of time of seven p.m., even though we had grown somewhat accustomed to adapting to Greek time, tending to dine late in the evening after the sun had gone down. Although it was still early for us the taverna was beginning to fill up with tourists, though there was no sign of any Greek diners, including Spiros. Any Greek holiday-makers would likely still be frolicking in the sea, considering this time of day to be mid-after-noon.

Whilst the coastal taverna Marigold had chosen was definitely more up-market than our local it still had a rustic air, trees with white-washed trunks providing welcome shade for the outdoor seating. The main village road snaking past the taverna was closed to traffic in the evenings, sparing us from noxious fumes belched from passing Greek vehicles only fit for the scrapheap, and safeguarding waiters from hit and runs. The street separating the taverna from the beach bustled with a constant prome-nade of tourists preening in their holiday finery and dodging the local youngsters weaving with reckless abandon between them on bicycles. The taverna was a perfect spot for people watching. Although Marigold personally preferred a nearby establishment with linen tablecloths and proper wine glasses which elevated it from ta-verna to fancy restaurant status, she was reluctant to risk taking Violet Burke there in case my mother's outrageous antics showed us up.

The family were gathered around a long table, Violet Burke sandwiched between Benjamin and Sampaguita. I slipped into the seat next to Marigold and opposite my mother, leaving Spiros to claim the seat at the head of the table when he finally turned up. Cynthia reassured Barry that she was feeling fine now: arriving at the tour office that morning she had felt a tad queasy so elected to spend the day in the office rather than risking hurling over the holiday-makers on the coach to Vathia. Biting my tongue I restrained myself from mentioning that her apparent hangover had left Rodney in Tiffany's incompetent hands; at least the unsatisfactory customer surveys would make mine look good in comparison.

"Ooh would you look at the price of them scallops, it's shocking," my mother vented, peering at the menu over the rectangular glasses perched on the end of her nose.

"Seafood does tend to be quite pricey in Greece even though we are by the sea," I told her.

"What are you on about? Since when did scallops come out of the sea?" my mother argued obtusely. "They must have seen you coming when you chose this place to eat. I'd be the laughing stock of Warrington if I tried to charge more than 20p for a scallop in the chippy."

"Of course scallops come out of the sea Granny, they are molluscs from the same family as oysters and clams," Benjamin assured her.

"Vi is obviously on about chip shop scallops, not the fancy ones you get here," Barry said, adding in a wistful tone, "I was always quite partial to a chip shop scallop with a few dubs on the side."

"Now I think about it I have come across dubs, Barry," I said with a shudder. I remembered arguing with the jumped-up Greek-Cypriot owner of a chippy with delusions of Michelin star abilities about his unhygienic practice of serving up bits of suspect looking bits of batter that ought by rights to have been chucked in the bin rather than be featured on his menu. Luckily I managed to dodge the bucket of batter he threw at me when I awarded him a paltry two stars on the hygiene scale, though I wouldn't have put it past him to scoop up and fry the contents of said bucket once I had made my escape. I certainly made a point of avoiding dubs after that unfortunate encounter.

"A chip shop scallop is a deep fried slice of battered potato," Barry announced to everyone. Humouring my mother, he added, "I've never come across them in Greece Vi, they don't know what they're missing."

"I'll knock up some batter in the morning and fry some up for your breakfast lad," my mother promised, ignoring the withering look that Marigold fired in her direction, having banned fry-up breakfasts as unhealthy. Barry's objections couldn't win Marigold round even when he claimed they would never have created a successful marketing slogan out of 'go to work on a bowl of Greek yoghurt.' Marigold refused to tolerate dissent, pointing out that our breakfast table positively heaved under an array of healthy goodies including fresh eggs, taverna bread baked in an outdoor wood oven, yoghurt, and fruit from the garden.

"A fry-up would set me up better for a day of manual labour," Barry had argued.

"Oh don't be such a wuss Barry, Athena sends Vangelis out to do manual labour with nothing more than a Greek coffee and a cigarette to sustain him," Marigold had retorted. I considered that explained Vangelis' proclivity for downing tools to down cheese pies at every opportunity.

Sampaguita's expression changing from polite confusion to positive radiance heralded the late arrival of Spiros. The undertaker was back to his usual cheery self as he went round the table greeting everyone and depositing double kisses.

"Here, there's no need to be so forward," Violet Burke objected as Spiros closed in on her. Spiros recoiled at the last moment, his bushy eyebrows almost meeting as his brow furrowed. He was no doubt repulsed when his nasal senses were assaulted by my mother's unique choice of chippy oil mosquito repellent.

When Benjamin introduced him to Adam, Spiros proclaimed, "Ah, you are the handsome homosexual boyfriend. We Greeks invented the homosexuality."

"Is he another gay one like the boys?" Violet Burke hissed loud enough for everyone at the nearby tables to overhear, attracting some inquisitive looks from the other diners.

"The uncle is perhaps the homosexual but I am the unbending," Spiros retorted.

"Straight," I corrected, before telling Violet Burke that Spiros and Sampaguita were courting.

"If he's not gay why does he keep kissing men?" Violet Burke tactlessly blurted.

"Mother, it's just the customary way of greeting between friends in Greece," I explained.

"Well I'm sure that goes down a treat in the flu season," my mother scoffed before turning to Sampaguita and asking, "Do they carry on with all that kissing lark where you come from?"

"No, we Filipinos are more reserved, we prefer to shake the hand. We have the traditional 'mano' greeting to show respect for the elderly, if you give me your hand I will show you," Sampaguita offered, taking my mother's hand and bringing it up to touch her forehead. "That is the sign in Filipino culture that you have honoured me by blessing me with the wisdom of your age."

"That's much more acceptable than all this going round kissing random strangers," my mother decreed. "I like a culture that reveres its elders. Now can we get on with ordering some food before I fade away from starvation?"

"I don't think there's much chance of that," Cynthia snapped, running a critical eye over my mother's bulbous shape. Fortunately Violet

Burke was too busy shuffling out of her cardigan to register the snide remark. My mother's cardigan disrobing revealed sturdy bare arms that would have done a shot-put thrower proud, but the rolls of flab bulging from her under arms made me reflect that Marigold had a point when she insisted we eschew breakfast fry-ups. I hoped that running to fat was not an inherited characteristic.

"The *mezedes* are the excellent here, let us to order the selection for the table," Spiros suggested.

"Does this messy stuff come with chips?" Violet Burke barked.

"*Mezedes* mother, it's a selection of Greek appetisers which we usually order with a plate of chips."

"Well don't forget to tell them to leave off that horrible green stuff."

"*Horis rigano,*" I explained to Spiros, advising him to order the chips without oregano.

Everyone except Violet Burke was happy for Spiros to order on our behalf, voicing individual preferences for his selection to include Kalamata olives, *tzatziki, taramasolata, fava, saganaki, gavros* and *tiganita keftedakia.*

"I hope he knows what he's doing, I need

something substantial after that sorry excuse for a lunch," Violet Burke said.

"Don't worry, Spiros has ordered some fried meatballs and two plates of chips," I assured her.

As we waited for the food to arrive I relaxed, allowing the table chatter to wash over me. Spiros appeared to be whispering sweet nothings to a blushing Sampaguita, whilst Benjamin was deep in conversation with his granny. Marigold caught my attention, saying she wished I could have taken a fortnight off work so I'd be able to spend more time with our visitors the following week. I pointed out that I'd been lucky to secure a week off in the height of the holiday season, reminding her that Benjamin had promised to take up the brunt of entertaining my mother and that my repping job was only part-time.

The waiter began to deposit plates of delicious looking *meze* on our table and everyone began to tuck in. Two large bowls of *horiatiko salata* were met with a groan from Violet Burke, complaining "we already had salad swimming in oil for lunch." Explaining that most Greek meals included a healthy salad I passed her the platter of fried meatballs. I attempted to hide my amusement at Spiros' affronted expression when she claimed the *keftedes* as her personal meal, rather than something for everyone to share, quietly asking the waiter to bring another serving for the table.

Benjamin exclaimed in delight as he tasted the *horta*. My mother took one look at the dish of boiled wild greens glistening with a squeeze of fresh lemon; without even sampling it she decreed that nothing would induce her to eat "that nasty spinach stuff."

"It isn't spinach, it is *horta*," I told her. As I explained what *horta* is and how it is a popular staple of the Greek diet her face adopted a vinegarish expression of incredulity.

"Can't you afford proper tinned vegetables?" Violet Burke spat. "I can't believe that you eat weeds, I bet you didn't have such strange foreign notions back in England."

"I suppose technically they are weeds, but only in so much that it is vegetation that grows wild," I protested. "*Horta* is a mix of wild greens, but whilst I have picked up the Greek names for some of them I'm not familiar enough with botanical terms to be exactly sure what *lapatho, kafkalida, boratzi,* and *pikralida* are in English."

"*Pikralida* is a dandelion," Marigold volunteered.

"The pair of you need your heads examining, sitting there telling me you pay good money to eat dandelions," my mother sneered. "There's dandelions growing between the cobbles in the alley behind the chippy, they sprout up next to the bins, but you wouldn't catch me cooking them up. If you're that stuck on having veggies wouldn't you rather have something a bit more substantial like a nice boiled cabbage?"

"Well we don't really tend to collect wild greens to cook at home, but they are a tasty addition to a restaurant meal," Marigold piped up defensively, at least having the grace to blush. In point of fact my wife had put her foot down after the first time I had experimentally gathered *horta* and boiled it up in the kitchen, complaining the ghastly smell lingered for weeks. It was now considered a banned foodstuff, along with the breakfast fry-ups.

"I bet if Victor brought you home a nice bunch of carnations from the flower shop you'd probably cook them instead of putting them in a vase on the mantelpiece," my mother mocked.

"That's rather a moot point since the only flower shops we've seen have been full of plastic blooms," I retorted.

"Don't tell us you expect us to use plastic flowers to decorate the wedding venue?" Adam screeched in genuine horror.

Chapter 11

A Neapolitan Scoop

How about the five of us take a mooch around the gift shops to walk off our dinner," Marigold suggested. Barry and Cynthia had snuck away early from the taverna, heading back to Meli when Cynthia began to feel a tad queasy again. Following their example Spiros and Sampaguita pulled a disappearing act, Spiros telling me he wanted to enjoy a romantic stroll in the moonlight with his fragrant Filipana flower.

"I'm always up for a bit of retail therapy," Adam agreed.

"I could do with getting some sandals, my feet are straining at the bit and sweating something terrible in these lace-ups," Violet Burke said.

"Come on Vi, I know just the place," Marigold encouraged, never one to miss an opportunity to wreak havoc with my credit card.

Whilst Violet Burke attempted to prise her swollen feet into traditional hand-crafted leather sandals, Adam snapped up a set of authentic *komboloi* worry beads, voicing the opinion they gave him a distinctly Greek air, before turning his attention to a chess set featuring positively indecent phallic pieces. I cringed in embarrassment as he showed the priapic carvings to my mother, surprised when she emitted a bawdy laugh and a comment not fit to repeat in these pages.

Marigold, determined to make a dent in my credit card, wanted to splash out on an eye-wateringly expensive set of traditional demitasse coffee cups as a wedding present for Barry and Cynthia. I pointed out that we had already splurged enough cash on their wedding reception and honeymoon. I felt relief when my mother sneered at the delicate cups Marigold had been eyeing, proclaiming they weren't even big enough to hold a tea bag. Her timely intervention at least spared my credit card. Marigold settled instead to treating my mother to a bottle of olive oil body lotion that didn't break the bank, saying she couldn't help but notice once the cardie came off that Violet Burke's elbows were riddled with dry patches.

Although Violet Burke had announced that she wasn't one for shopping for fripperies I couldn't help but notice that she seemed quite drawn to a display of *matiasma*, her attention transfixed by the traditional jewellery fashioned in the form of watching blue eyes. I explained to her that each blue *mati* piece represented protective talismans thought to ward off the evil eye. Fully expecting her to scoff at the notion of such superstitious nonsense she surprised me by appearing quite enamoured by the idea.

"I could do with one of them, that Mrs Billings who comes in for fried haddock every Friday is forever giving me the evil eye."

With such a strong endorsement I immediately treated my mother to a blue *mati* brooch. She was so touched by the gesture that she insisted on pinning it to her cardie immediately, preening with pleasure at the traditional decorative piece. "That was nice of you dear, I don't think she has many nice things," Marigold said approvingly.

"Come on Granny, I'll treat us all to an ice cream," Benjamin offered.

"I'm going to think I'm on holiday if everyone keeps fussing me," Violet Burke replied with an indulgent smile.

"You are on your hols Granny," Benjamin reminded her.

My four companions dithered over the tempting selection at the ice cream parlour, spoilt for choice. Since the *tzatziki* I'd eaten earlier had been a bit heavy on the garlic I opted for a refreshing lemon sorbet to cleanse my palate, whilst Marigold and Benjamin indulged in their favourite and predictable pistachio, and Adam went for chocolate.

"I suppose I could force a slice of Viennetta down if you twist my arm," Violet Burke grudgingly admitted.

"Mother, they don't sell processed food, all the ice-cream here is handmade on the premises."

"I quite fancy a nice soft scoop of Wall's Neapolitan."

"Take a seat with the others and I'll get you the nearest thing," I promised, ordering her a scoop of vanilla, strawberry and chocolate.

The five of us claimed a table overlooking the street. Settling back with our ice creams we had a perfect view of the sea, its seemingly immense blackness only broken by the reflection of lights on the water from distant fishing boats. We watched the holidaymakers tripping by, moseying in and out of the gift shops and the cafe bars lining the seafront. Spiros and Sampaguita walked past, so entwined in one another they didn't even notice us.

"This is excellent," Benjamin said, savouring his scoop of pistachio.

"It's hardly surprising since Greece is the original birth-place of ice cream," I boasted. "The ancient Greeks first came up with the delicious treat by mixing fruit and honey into snow."

"Come off it, you're pulling our legs, where would they be getting snow from in this hot place?" my mother scoffed.

"Although Greece is blessed with a hot climate it does actually get snow in the mountains and even in Athens," I assured her.

"The peaks of Taygetos were snow-capped this winter, such a beautiful sight," Marigold said. "We even had a few frosty mornings up in Meli."

"Are you enjoying your ice cream Granny?" Benjamin asked, always mindful of her well-being.

"Well it's not as much to my taste as Wall's, but it will do lad," Violet Burke replied. "Do you know I can still remember the first time I tasted ice cream, it was in Blackpool back in 1949?"

"I've not been to Blackpool for years," Benjamin said. "I remember Mum and Dad taking me to see the illuminations when I was a child."

"Ooh, I wish I'd known you when you were a nipper," my mother sighed, ruffling Benjamin's hair fondly.

"We haven't been to Blackpool for years, Marigold prefers Southport..."

"Well it's much more up-market," Marigold said.

"So what took you to Blackpool in 1949?" I asked my mother.

"We went for the weekend to see the illuminations; it was the first time they'd been on since before the war. I had my first ever donkey ride, and we did the pier and the tower. Me and Ernest queued up for ages outside Notarianni's sea-side parlour for a scoop of vanilla, ooh it was good," Violet Burke said. Scraping the last of the ice cream from the bowl her eyes narrowed pensively; she was seemingly lost to her memories.

"So who was Ernest, was he your beau?" Benjamin blurted.

"He was my first husband," Violet Burke revealed, shocking the four of us to attention since it was the first we'd ever heard of his existence. During her previous visit Violet Burke had only mentioned one husband, Lionel, though I recalled that he had been husband number three. There were gaping gaps in my knowledge of my mother's personal history that I was keen to plug.

I gripped Marigold's hand tightly as an icy flow surged through my veins and my imagination went into overdrive. I reflected that if Violet Burke had been a married woman in 1949 there may be a possibility that this Ernest chap could be my father if she'd been carrying on with him before the end of the war. My mother had told me that she wasn't absolutely certain that Vic, the dodgy soap salesman from Crewe with a hygiene obsession and a nice line in patter, was definitely my father. It struck me that she had simply stuck a pin in his name after ruling out Ulysses, the arse end Charlie black trumpet player from Mississippi, and Donnie, the nice Jewish boffin from Brooklyn, as actual contenders for siring me. Since she had obviously been loose with her favours perhaps Ernest was a possibility she had simply overlooked. I realised that I was clutching at straws, but it pained me to think I was fathered by an irresponsible army deserter who apparently couldn't even be bothered to fake limp on the same leg with any consistency.

Marigold squeezed my hand, obviously in tune with the turn of my thoughts. We both leant forward, hanging on every word as Violet Burke told us about Ernest.

"He was my first husband but I didn't really know Ernest that well, we got wed a couple of years after the war ended. He was younger than me, handsome, but a bit wet behind the ears. I figured he might get on in life because he had a head for figures, and I don't mean just mine, though it was pretty cracking," Violet Burke said with what I think she intended to be a saucy wink.

"I bet you were definitely a looker Granny," Benjamin encouraged.

"There's no denying that with my statuesque figure, my shapely pins and my flaming red hair, I turned a few heads," she said with no trace of modesty.

"You were telling us about Ernest," I reminded her.

"Well like I say I thought he might get on because he had a steady job as a bank clerk, but then he only went and got himself drafted not long after his eighteenth birthday. They sent him overseas so I never got to see him on leave. I thought he'd be all worldly and not so wet after being sent abroad, but the daft dipstick only went and picked up a nasty dose of..."

A bout of coughing interrupted her tale as the ice cream went down the wrong way. Marigold and I exchanged horrified expressions, certain that my mother was going to reveal that her first husband Ernest picked up a nasty dose of venereal disease, the embarrassing condition which made a laughing stock of the original initials I'd been lumbered with.

After Benjamin thumped her on the back and Adam passed her a glass of water, she regained her composure, continuing her sorry saga. "Now where was I?"

"You were telling us that Ernest caught a

nasty dose of something we suspect is unmentionable," I prompted.

"Since when has the mumps been unmentionable?" Violet Burke retorted. "Mind you the mumps did have a horrible complication in his case, poor Ernest ended up with testicular atrophy."

The boys and I winced in genuine sympathy, whilst Marigold simply looked baffled. When the penny finally dropped her mouth formed a perfect 'O' and she blushed.

"Of course I knew nothing about it until that weekend away in Blackpool because it was the first time I'd seen him in nearly two years. I have to say I was really taken aback that after his conscription abroad he was still right wet behind the ears. I might have been able to overlook what a wet blanket he was but that nasty dose he went and caught didn't half put the damper on any bedroom activity. I hadn't signed up for marriage with a man who went and got shrunken appendages, it wasn't half off-putting."

"Vi really, I don't think this is appropriate talk in front of the boys," Marigold remonstrated.

"Boys, the lads are in their thirties and not

exactly a pair of vestal virgins. I doubt I could say anything to shock them, did you see that mucky chess set they had their hands on earlier?"

A stifled titter from the table behind us drew my attention and I fired off one of Marigold's best withering looks in their direction, only giving my mother my full attention again when she continued: "The marriage didn't last for long after that weekend in Blackpool; it was like flogging a dead horse."

"So you didn't know Ernest back in 1944?" I asked pointlessly, having calculated he would have only been fifteen when I was conceived. I would need to extract some more excruciatingly embarrassing details from my mother if I wanted to make certain the dodgy soap salesman was my father.

Chapter 12

Going Round in Circles

I endured a restless night following our evening on the coast, a touch of heartburn from indulging in too much *tzatziki* and the persistent itching from my latest mosquito bite preventing me from sleeping. Tossing and turning, careful not to disturb Marigold as I glugged the chalky contents directly from a bottle of Gaviscon, my tortured thoughts repeatedly returned to my still questionable paternity. Prior to my first ever meeting with Violet Burke the previous year I had never wasted a moment speculating about my paternal origins: what-ever thoughts I had regarding being abandoned in a bucket revolved around my absconded mother. It was only since becoming acquainted with my mother that curiosity regarding my fa-ther had been ignited.

In the midnight hour my thoughts turned to the possibility of tracing my father. For all I knew the limping Casanova could still be alive and may even have spawned a veritable collec-tion of buckets with his sweet soap-talking ways. Rather than being an abandoned orphan I may have a collection of stranger siblings, though I hoped just in the sense of strange to me rather than actually strange as in odd.

I was just on the verge of losing myself in blissful oblivion when the irritating and persis-tent bark of a dog jolted me into wakefulness. Thumping the pillow I made the decision to broach the subject with Violet Burke. I decided it would be prudent to talk with her privately without the rest of the family putting their two penn'orth worth in. Our imminent day out on Pegasus was likely to throw up an opportunity for some alone time with her whilst the rest of the family enjoyed a swim. I very much doubted Violet Burke would be persuaded to lower her bulbous frame into the sea, rather imagining that she would consider the water as nothing more than a convenient larder for fish, their ultimate destination the chip shop fryer.

By the time the first crow of the rooster sounded I was up and showered with a steaming mug of freshly brewed coffee in hand. Barry, to my surprise, was once again snoring away on the sofa: I smiled to myself, speculating that he was saving himself for his wedding night. In no mood to put up with my mother until the caffeine had kicked in I headed out to the garden at the first sound of her distinctive tread, leaving her to brew her own PG Tips.

It appeared I wasn't the only one making an early start as Guzim was already on his hands and knees, deep in chicken muck. I was ready to tackle him about the subject of hanging his underwear across my garden with gay abandon, having practiced the necessary phrase, though I must confess to taking the coward's way out by pinning the objection on Marigold.

"*I ynaika mou den aresei na to kremata ston kipo,*" I told him, saying my wife didn't like him hanging his things in the garden.

"*Yiati? Einai mono roucha,*" Guzim retorted, asking why, it is only clothes.

"*Einai esoroucha,*" I said, pointing out it was underwear. I was rather taken aback with Guzim's response of *etsi*, meaning so, having rather expected he would meekly capitulate to my bidding to remove the offending garments from my garden. Unprepared for his standing up to me I groped around in my mind for the Greek word for sensitive, blurting out "*I ynaika mou einai evaisthitos arakas.*"

"*Ti?*" Guzim snapped 'what?' before muttering some incomprehensible Greek under his breath. The only word I picked out was *trelos*, meaning I was crazy. I considered it a bit much that my part-time gardener was mumbling insults about his employer until it suddenly dawned on me that I had just randomly confused my wife with 'sensitive peas.' My chat with Nikos about mushy peas must have lingered in my brain, making me muddle my words.

Attempting to reclaim my dignity I mentally ran the words through my head before asking him to put his underwear somewhere else, not in my garden. "*Valte ta esoroucha sas kapou allou, ochi ston kipo mou.*"

I felt we were going round in circles when Guzim again demanded "*yiati*" why, and I once again told him my wife didn't like it. I struggled to understand Guzim's response because his Greek tended to speed up when he was consumed with righteous indignation. He seemed to be twittering on that he didn't like to be forced to look at enormous bras whilst working in the chicken run. I couldn't make sense of his complaints until he pointed to the shutters outside the guest room, festooned with what appeared to be a double-barrelled brassiere of gargantuan proportions and a reinforced girdle. It appeared that Violet Burke had done a spot of hand washing, hanging her anything but smalls out to dry with no thought to the overly delicate sensibilities of any revolted Albanian shed dwellers who may be confronted by the offending sight, whilst scooping up chicken muck with their bare hands.

"*Anypomonoume gia to gamo*?" I said, abruptly changing the subject and asking if he was looking forward to the wedding.

Guzim threw his head back and clucked, indicating a negative response. His tone was most definitely put out when he voiced the complaint that he would have to go to the expense of buying a new shirt for the occasion. Eager to placate him I promised to rummage through my wardrobe to see if I could find a suitable cast-off. I can't be one hundred percent certain but I think what he said loosely translated to 'see if you can't find me some underwear too since your wife objects to mine.' I chose to ignore him; he was hardly likely to lower his trousers and expose his shabby underwear at the wedding.

Chapter 13

A Dolphin in the Ship Canal

Delighted to have secured a free day out on Pegasus for my family in return for my rudimentary translating skills, I was thrilled that we wouldn't be crammed in amongst the tourist hordes. As an extra bonus, instead of shelling out for tickets I was to receive an under the table payment for my trouble. The boat had been privately chartered by three French divers who planned to chart the course of the cold water springs off the coast of the village we had dined in the previous evening. Instead of having to drive all the way up to town to embark on the boat as I did when repping on the lazy day cruise, I simply had to drive Marigold, my mother and the boys down to the coast. Saying that, it proved a bit of a squeeze cramming the five of us into the Punto because my family insisted on carting along so much superfluous beach paraphernalia that anyone would think we were off on a fortnight's cruise.

"I can't possibly manage without my styling products," Adam said in a peevish tone when I suggested his vanity case was an unnecessary addition. "Have you any idea of the damage sea water will do my hair? It will end up all brittle and parched if I don't have my products to hand."

"I didn't realise Adam was so vain," I whispered to Benjamin, glad that I was of the generation that had escaped the current self-obsessed trend that had men plucking or waxing every hair from their body whilst pampering and styling whatever was left on the top of their head. Fortunately I still boast a full head of healthy hair that I maintain with minimal fuss and baby shampoo, though it is well overdue a discreet application of Grecian 2000 since I haven't been able to locate a supply locally.

"Oh, he isn't really vain, it's just that his hair is a bit of a sensitive topic since he noticed how quickly his hairline has started to recede." I struggled to keep a straight face; Benjamin's choice of words reminded me of a frightfully pretentious and vain maître d'hôtel who also considered his premature baldness a sensitive topic and resorted to using Toppic hair building fibres to thicken his barnet. The jumped up waiter tried to pass himself off as French, hoping to cash in on the extra cachet, but his French pronunciation carried a distinctive Mancunian twang and the Toppic made it appear as though he had a thick coating of dandruff.

Benjamin, oblivious that my thoughts had drifted, continued to speak. "I'm lucky to have inherited your genes and don't need to worry about the onset of early pattern hair loss."

My son's words struck a chord; safe in the knowledge of his own paternity he had a fair idea of what to expect from ageing, whilst at his age I had been clueless if I was the product of dodgy gene stock. My recent discovery of Violet Burke had finally solved the mystery of one half of my inherited gene conundrum, but even as I approached my sixtieth year the other half of the equation still remained elusive.

"We need to put the picnic basket somewhere cool," Marigold reminded me. My wife had surpassed herself preparing a lovely light lunch of salad, dips, crusty bread and fruit, a perfect selection that wouldn't weigh us down in the water.

"Will someone shove my beach bag in the boot?" Violet Burke interrupted.

Amazed at the size of her bulky bag I reminded her that we were only going out for the day.

"I know but there's nothing worse than sitting round in a damp cossie with seaweed and sand in your gusset, so I packed a spare, as well as a change of clothes and undies," my mother said, immediately conjuring up an unwelcome vision of the gargantuan reinforced bra hanging from the shutters. Recalling Guzim's aggrieved reaction I wondered if it had been genuine or perhaps a tad manipulative; after all, the Albanian shed dweller had form.

"Your mother threw our best bath towels in her bag, do you suppose we've time to stop and buy her a new beach towel?" Marigold hissed in my ear.

"No, we're going to be late for the off as it is

if we don't get going at once," I said, urging everyone to get in the car. "Don't forget that I am technically working and it won't do to tar my professional reputation by being tardy."

Finally with everyone wedged into the car Marigold piped up from the back seat, "I must say Victor I am rather looking forward to meeting your *Kapetanios* after hearing so much about him, he certainly sounds like an interesting personality."

I groaned inwardly at her words, realising I may have somewhat embellished Vasos' character whilst playing down his tendency to be half-cut most of the time. Still I felt it prudent to warn the family that they would likely be on the receiving end of some random English words from the Captain, but they should consider them little better than gibberish since he had no clue to their meaning.

"I think it is marvellous how you've adapted to Greek life, taking on repping is such a departure from your previous career," Benjamin said.

"It has its challenges," I replied. "But I do enjoy imparting my knowledge of the area and its history to tourists with a genuine interest."

"Your father had his head buried in one

dusty old tome after another to make himself an authority," Marigold said.

"Well I hope he isn't going to bore us all silly with a history lecture today. I can't be doing with know-it-all's pontificating, too much in love with the sound of their own voice," my mother said.

"On the contrary I will spare you anything fact related, I just want you all to enjoy a pleasant day out on the boat," I replied sniffily.

Picking our path with care we tripped through the horde of children hurling themselves with gay abandon from the harbour wall into the sea. It was a popular spot for the local youngsters to perfect their dives and back flip techniques, taking a morning dip before heading home to avoid the dangerous rays of the midday sun. I imagined overly protective Greek Mamas' fussing over them, keeping them in darkened rooms with the shutters closed against the sun during the height of the day when the foreign tourists prostrated themselves on the beach, slowly roasting their white skin until it resembled a slab of cooked meat from Nikos' grill.

Recalling the days of Benjamin's childhood, I couldn't imagine him willingly submitting to an enforced siesta, but the Greeks had their children well-trained. Their siesta habit accounted for their late night presence in the tavernas and the energy they displayed when playing outside at an hour way past my own bedtime. I often considered our decision to move to a remote mountain village had been an eminently sensible one since it spared us the sound of shrieking children playing in the streets, the occasional presence of noisy youngsters visiting elderly grandparents bearable because it was such a rare disturbance.

Pegasus was docked in the harbour, the gang-plank conveniently down, but there was no sign of Captain Vasos or his mute side-kick Sami. Shepherding my family on-board I encouraged them to make themselves comfortable on the deck whilst I inspected the vessel to make sure everything was ship-shape for the private charter. It appeared as though Sami had already been busy with the mop and bucket, the lavatory cubicle for once free of floating toilet paper. I directed Marigold to the hold with the picnic basket as the food needed refrigerating before it turned in the heat, but my mother grabbed the basket, insisting she would see to it, muttering something about Marigold collapsing under the weight.

"It's nice to see Vi getting into the spirit of things and mucking in," Marigold said. I was relieved that my wife wasn't finding my mother's visit too much of an ordeal this time.

I pointed my mother in the direction of the toilet when she asked where she could change into her swimming costume, not bothering to ask why she hadn't simply put it on under her clothes that morning.

"Shouldn't that technically be the head, rather than the toilet, in nautical terms?" Adam asked.

"Well I'm not sure if it's the same on a Greek boat," I replied uncertainly. The occasional Greek passengers had only ever asked directions to the *toualeta*, never the *kefali*.

A cry of "bonjour" from the gangplank heralded the arrival of the French divers and I rushed to greet them and welcome them onboard, cursing Vasos for his absence. Henri, the only one of the three French men who spoke any English, introduced me to his companions Jules and Gustave. Even though they were a fit looking bunch in their twenties and thirties they struggled to haul their diving equipment onto the boat, weighed down with wet suits, scuba tanks, submersible pressure gauges, underwater cameras and a myriad of other essential apparatus necessary for their professional dive which would hopefully provide some useful scientific insights.

"I am appreciating you coming today to translate because the language barrier meant I could not communicate with the captain and it was impossible to get a word out of his bosom," Henri said.

Raising a quizzical eyebrow I wondered if it was some peculiar French kink that led Henri to expect to have a conversation with Vasos' chest. I felt rather stupid when it belatedly dawned on me that Henri was referring to the boat's bosun, his imperfect English leading him to confuse bosom with bosun, the latter a role he must have relegated in his mind to Sami.

"You won't get a word out of Sami because unfortunately he is mute," I explained.

"It is odd that he is so silent if he is open to debate," Henri pondered.

"No, not moot, mute, he is incapable of speaking," I clarified, thinking I was certainly going to have to earn my wages for my translating skills if I had to decipher many more malapropisms, and that was before we even got around to my converting Henri's English into comprehensible Greek for Vasos' benefit.

"I must say I appreciate your invitation to bring my family along, I'll try to keep them out of your way," I said to Henri.

"It is no problem, the boat is very big and we will be working under water. I will only call on you to tell the Captain what we need."

"Let me get you some help to haul that equipment on board," I offered, calling Benjamin and Adam over to lend a hand. A wave of relief washed over me when Adam started chatting away to the new arrivals in their own language. I would be able to call on him as a backup if necessary if cornered by either Gustave or Jules. My own mastery of the French language was rather limited to the names of a few Cordon Bleu dishes since my illustrious career as a public health inspector had necessitated my close proximity to many a veloute and espagnole. I supposed that peppering my conversation with references to coq au vin and beef bourguignon would only serve to make me appear to be a jabbering half-wit, and a hungry one at that.

As soon as all the dive equipment was safely stowed on board Captain Vasos and Sami finally put in a late appearance, Vasos explaining their absence by saying they'd gone off for coffee. My cynic detector went into overdrive as I calculated their arrival was impeccably timed to ensure they'd avoided getting roped into lugging the bulky apparatus aboard. I couldn't help but notice that the three fastidiously groomed French men recoiled at the first rather ripe whiff of the *Kapetanios* emitting a strong aroma of ouzo and sweat when he met them with a jovial greeting, proclaiming "Hello, good towel." Only Henri raised a bemused eyebrow, his two companions impervious to the fact that Vasos' use of English may as well be complete gibberish.

Gustave and Jules frowned when Sami scuttled past them without responding to their greeting, a dog end hanging from his mouth and his shoulders slumped in characteristic hangdog posture. There were excited French accented exclamations of "Ah" when Henri presumably relayed the information that I had given him regarding Sami's muteness.

Before introducing Vasos to the family I concentrated on business, relaying the divers' plans to Vasos, telling him they wished to stop at three particular spots to chart the underwater cold springs and the state of the sea bed. I directed Vasos to where they wanted to make their first dive, a few kilometres from shore: fortunately the diving spots were mapped out on a nautical chart that didn't require any translation. With Vasos fully conversant with the divers' instructions the three French men disappeared below to change into their wetsuits. I took the opportunity to introduce Marigold and the boys to Vasos before he kick-started the engine, the Captain immediately charming my wife by declaring in English, "Hello yes beautiful, beautiful." Fortunately he hadn't yet downed enough ouzo to declare that he loved her.

Vasos skilfully steered Pegasus out of the harbour and we all waved cheerily to the children thrashing around in the water. As the boat followed its course into the open sea the toilet door was thrust violently open, revealing Violet Burke in all her glory. My mother presented the most extraordinary sight, clad in the most bizarre swimsuit that appeared to be some prewar relic. The costume was fashioned in navy, broad horizontal white stripes unflatteringly accentuating her girth, with seemingly reinforced moulded bra cups holding her ample bosom immovably in place. The costume morphed into a skirt flaring out atop modesty preserving matching shorts ending at her knees: I imagined the inbuilt shorts had once been thigh hugging, but were now merely baggy. A rubber swimming cap festooned with multi-coloured floral petals, a rubber strap securing it in place and cutting into her double chin, completed the outfit.

Whilst I gazed at my mother, lost for words in gob-smacked amazement, Marigold leapt into the breach, saying "You look very nautical Vi, is that a retro costume?"

"No, it's an original, I got it for that trip to Blackpool back in 1949 but it's not had much wear. There's not much call for a cossie in Warrington since the ship canal got too mucky to swim in. Now when I was a girl we used to cool off in the canal but it's a veritable cesspit of germs these days, littered with dead bodies and shopping trollies I shouldn't wonder."

"I imagine it is a petri dish for breeding bacteria," I said with a shudder, recalling that nothing would have induced me into taking a dip in the Manchester Ship Canal.

"And there's not only dead things swimming about in the canal, can you believe that only a couple of years back it was invaded by a dolphin, can you credit it?" my mother continued. "It's not natural."

Recalling that I had read about a bottle nosed dolphin floundering about in the ship canal in 2000, unable to find its way back to the sea, I could indeed credit it. It seemed that some of my mother's outrageous statements weren't actually quite as outlandish as I had first supposed, but rather gleaned from tabloid headlines.

The conversation was interrupted by the three French divers now kitted out in full diving gear trooping past us, ready to launch themselves into the water when Vasos reached the first scheduled stop. As they sorted through their equipment Violet Burke settled down on the wooden bench seat edging the deck and proceeded to fill us all in on a slice of ship canal history, despite her previous vocal objections to hearing dull historical facts. Actually Vi proved quite the story teller, regaling us with information that I found utterly fascinating, particularly since it included a snippet of family history.

My mother told us that the sight of the divers kitted out in full diving gear put her in mind of her late grandfather, Enos Blossom.

Originally employed as one of the thousands of navvies engaged in the construction of the Manchester Ship Canal in the late nineteenth century, Enos worked his way up, training for and securing a position as one of the divers. She described an old sepia photograph of him that had adorned the family mantelpiece, Enos clad in a diving suit that had more of a resemblance to a hazmat or astronaut suit than the slim line diving gear being modelled by the young French men on the boat.

"It was a hazardous business doing underwater checks in the big ditch. Even though he was always a bit on the paranoid side about getting a blockage in the hose that fed him oxygen, he never let on that he was prone to attacks of hyperventilating, in case his work mates made fun of him being a hypochondriac," she said bluntly.

"A fear of hypoxia would have been perfectly natural in the circumstances," I said, presuming that a lack of oxygen must have been a very real danger considering the rather primitive equipment available at the time.

"Well Enos Blossom was nowt if not practical. He just got on with the job because it was much better pay than what he'd earned as a navvy," my mother said.

"It must have been a huge task for manual labourers to dig out the canal, and those divers must have put their lives on the line," Adam said.

"My great-great-grandfather must have been a brave man to rise to the challenge. What was he like Granny?" Benjamin asked.

"I only knew him from the photo and of course he had to go and leave that enormous helmet on in the only picture. My Nan rued that helmet when she lost him, over and over she used to go on about the lazy ha'p'orth not bothering to take if off for the camera, moaning that his face was obscured in the one and only thing she had left of him. He caught a nasty dose of that Spanish flu back in 1919 and it finished him off, his lungs already being shot from all that work in the damp."

"How tragic, that means three generations of Buckets, sorry Blossoms, have grown up without knowing their grandfathers," Adam mused.

Adam's words reinforced my determination to have a quiet conversation with my mother and delve into the truth of my paternal origins. I could just imagine Benjamin's delight if I was able to locate a living Granddad for him.

Chapter 14

After a Tan

Approaching our first stop I stepped into the wheelhouse to catch up with Vasos. It was unusual to see the upper sun deck which backed onto the wheelhouse bereft of bodies, but I had deliberately steered Marigold onto the main deck to spare her the lecherous gaze of the goatish *Kapetanios.* Peering into the distance through binoculars, Vasos chugged back the contents of a water bottle. I crossed my fingers that the bottle actually contained water; it was way too early in the day for the Captain to be knocking back the ouzo.

"*Eimai kourasmenos*," Vasos sighed wearily, his general demeanour lacking his usual boisterousness as he complained he was tired, though I suspect he was likely more hungover than sleep deprived. "*Tha koimitho otan stamatisoume.*"

I reflected that his intention to sleep when we anchored would at least spare Marigold from any random declarations of love, though I had a sneaking feeling she would eagerly lap up the flattery; if nothing else Vasos was always sincere in his admiration of the ladies. The idea that he would attempt to charm Violet Burke was too preposterous for words, but I had no doubt that if Vasos was too drunk to know any better my mother was more than capable of putting the pongy Greek would-be Lothario in his place.

Vasos bellowed for Sami, instructing his side-kick to drop anchor. The moment the boat came to a halt Vasos collapsed wearily onto the bench, draping a fetid towel over his face. I was astonished by the remarkable speed in which he started snoring; personally I would never be able to drop off in such musty and unhygienic surroundings, littered with overflowing ashtrays and bits of old pie crust sprouting mould. Leaving him to it I re-joined my family who stood watch as the French men dived beneath the surface of the water. I looked forward to following their example and diving in since I was yet to swim from Pegasus, the repping rules preventing me from participating in tourist dips. Fortunately my family would not be deprived of my presence in the water since no such rules governed the brown envelope terms of that day's casual employment.

It was certainly a beautiful day for a swim, the cloudless sky an endless stretch of soft blue reflecting the temptingly turquoise water, as calm as a mill-pond. I considered I was a lucky man indeed as I admired the lovely image my wife presented making her way down the ladder, her Titian locks piled loosely on top of her head, her figure showed off to stunning advantage in a fetching floral one-piece.

When the boys stripped down to their swim shorts I wasn't particularly surprised to notice that Adam's chest appeared to have been plucked and waxed hairless since it was in keeping with his metrosexual obsession with moisturising and fussing over hair products. I proudly noted that Benjamin unashamedly sported a hairy chest like mine, though as yet his hadn't succumbed to grey. I must confess to vainly wishing that I could get my hands on a bottle of Grecian 2000, instead of having to settle for simply tidying up any strays with the nail scissors.

"Are you sure that ladder will take my weight?" my mother asked doubtfully.

"Yes, of course, it's very solid. Just hold on tight to the rungs and take your time," I said, calling down to Benjamin who was already in the sea to give his Granny a hand when she reached the bottom.

"Would you like a float to hold onto in the water?" I asked.

"Aye that would be grand. I might be a bit rusty at this swimming lark, but I expect it's like riding a bike."

Once in the sea I kept a concerned eye on my mother, noticing that she didn't like to venture too far from the safety of the ladder. When I drifted out of close range it was impossible to lose sight of her since her gaudy floral swim cap bobbed around like a warning buoy on the surface of the water. Nevertheless I was reassured to see Sami standing watch on the deck, ready to jump in to the rescue if necessary. After a while my mother appeared to relax, realising she did indeed have enough buoyancy to allow her bulbous body to float without sinking. A pleasant hour was passed in the water before I reminded everyone that it was a time for a top up of high factor sun protection before we roasted. Cynthia would no doubt go all bridezilla on us again if our red and peeling faces ruined the wedding photos.

As I rubbed sun cream into Marigold's back my mother produced a bottle of the olive oil she seemingly despised from the depths of her beach bag. Catching sight of my raised eyebrows she unapologetically said "I knew this stuff would come in useful for something besides constipation and unblocking ear wax." Before I could protest she began to liberally slather our premium extra virgin olive oil into her exposed flesh, saying "I might as well get a nice tan while I'm here, if nothing else it will make that Mrs Billings green when she comes in for her haddock a week on Friday." Since my mother clearly had the thick hide of a rhinoceros I decided it was pointless to proffer the unwanted advice that high factor sun cream would be a more prudent protective choice.

"That's the second time you've mentioned

Mrs Billings," Marigold said quizzically.

"The old bat cast aspersions on my cod."

I considered Mrs Billings must be made of strong mettle if she was willing to take on Violet Burke. It was satisfying to think that my mother would be able to put Mrs Billing's nose out of joint by boasting that she'd picked up a nice tan during her holiday in Greece.

"It's such a pity Barry couldn't join us today," Marigold said.

"He'll get a break on his honeymoon. It is more important for him to get the business established; after all he's a long way from retiring."

"He's taking a lot on, a new business, a new home and a new wife," Marigold admitted.

"Not to mention taking on Cynthia's vile cat, and all in a new country to boot," I agreed.

"Oh don't mention that revolting creature, Cynthia had a full on bridezilla moment yesterday. Can you believe she wanted to include it in the wedding, she thought its feelings might be hurt if she left it out."

"What on earth does she think she will do with a cat at the *Dimarcheio*? Rope it in as the ring bearer," I scoffed.

"Please don't say that to Cynthia, you don't

want to put any more daft ideas in her head," Marigold laughed. "I am looking forward to seeing Barry married and settled. I know he's always got us, but he deserves someone special to come home to at the end of each day."

"I couldn't have put it better myself," I concurred, relieved that the home Cynthia would be waiting for him in would no longer be ours.

Just then the three French divers resurfaced from their underwater exploration, working as a team to haul their equipment back on board. Henri approached me, saying they were ready to move onto the second spot where they hoped to take some samples of the limestone on the seabed. Taking my cue to wake the *Kapetanios* I stepped back up into the wheelhouse where Vasos was still sprawled out, his sweaty tee-shirt having ridden up to expose an unwelcome expanse of belly. His snoring had mercifully stopped, only the rise and fall of the towel covering his face indicating he hadn't suffocated under the fetid rag. Reluctant to put my hands on his sweating body to shake him awake I grabbed a bottle of water, pouring the contents over his stomach. Vasos immediately sprang to attention, no doubt used to rude awakenings during his long stint in the navy.

"Ora na fygo," I said, telling him it was time to go and stepping back to preserve my eardrums when Vasos bellowed for Sami.

The movement of the boat stirred a gentle and welcome breeze as we cut across the water, all too soon dropping anchor again. With the French men back underwater and my mother once again closeted in the toilet, the rest of us watched with interest as a small fishing boat approached, the blue and white painted wood creating a traditional Greek picture. As the boat edged closer we could see the name Ekaterina etched on the side and I wondered if the boat had been named for its owner's mother, a common custom. The old fisherman at the helm cut the engine as the boat grew level with Pegasus, removing his cap and waving it in greeting.

"Ela Sortiri, ela, ena ouzo mazi?" Vasos shouted down, asking if the fellow fancied an ouzo with him. Receiving a thumbs-up from the fisherman Vasos filled two glasses with ouzo before skilfully negotiating his way down the ladder, jumping into the smaller vessel without spilling a single drop. The peace of the day was shattered by their noisy banter, generously punctuated with unrepeatable expletives. After a good ten minutes Vasos swung back up the

ladder and the fishing boat punted away, the old fellow once again tipping his cap to us.

Settling down beside me Vasos clucked his tongue. "*Ta pragmata einai kaka ya ton Sotiri,*" he shouted, taking my family aback since they didn't realise that Vasos had adopted the habit of yelling at high volume to make himself heard over the din of the engine.

"*Yiati?*" I said, asking why things were bad for Sotiris, surprised when Vasos responded "*I varka einai ya ta skoupidia,*" meaning the boat is for the rubbish. Wondering if I had misunderstood the Captain since the fishing boat had certainly appeared to be in tip-top condition to my admittedly untrained eye, I asked him why it was destined for the rubbish: "*Yiati yia skoupidia?*"

"*Oi Germanoi lene oti prepei na to kopei,*" Vasos roared, emphasising his point with a rude gesture that I hoped wouldn't offend my wife's sensibilities. I stared at him in consternation, wondering how much truth there was to his words. Vasos had just told me that the Germans had decreed the fisherman's wooden fishing boat must be cut up. I was familiar enough with the disparaging local use of the word 'Germans' to understand that Vasos was referring to petty bureaucrats belonging to the European Union rather than to actual Germans, but it still made no sense why bureaucrats would dictate that a perfectly serviceable fishing boat should be relegated to the scrap heap, destroyed by being cut into unsalvageable pieces.

Throwing his hands up in frustration at my failure to grasp his meaning Vasos explained the situation in very loud, slow and precise Greek, couching his criticism as a deliberate German conspiracy in line with local opinion that the northern European nation had a stranglehold on power. With Marigold's help and the odd flick through the dictionary I finally began to make sense of the situation.

The old fisherman Sotiris was about to retire, but in order to get his hands on the compensation offered for hanging up his fishing nets he must comply with an EU directive to destroy his boat, a directive designed to stop overfishing of the Mediterranean. He was expected to not only give up the chance to fish at leisure during his retirement or to take his much loved boat out for a joy ride, but to deprive any aspiring fishermen amongst the younger generation of benefiting from his fishing experience, all in return for a paltry cash payment.

"But surely the old wooden fishing boats are an integral part of Greek tradition and culture," Marigold said, prompting Vasos to shout "*Ti?*"

With the help of the dictionary I offered Vasos a simplified translation of Marigold's words, "*alla ta skafi einai paradoskiaka,*" - but the boats are traditional.

"*Oi Germanoi ftynoun tin elliniki paradosi,*" Vasos retorted, spitting over the edge of the boat to emphasise his point that the Germans spat on Greek traditions, before stomping back to the wheelhouse to top up his glass of ouzo and grab another forty winks. I considered his hangover must be pretty bad; it wasn't like Vasos to be so unsociable, but at least his absence spared the women of our party from his fawning.

Chapter 15

A Picnic on Pegasus

I do hope that your mother is okay Victor, she seems to have been an absolute age in the loo," Marigold hissed.

"Well she is getting on," I pointed out.

"I'll just give her a knock to be on the safe side," Marigold said with a worried frown. Violet Burke responded to Marigold's tentative tap by opening the toilet door a smidgen, her hand shooting out to drag my wife inside the cubicle. Marigold emerged a few moments later, flushed red as she explained that Violet Burke had needed a hand unfurling the wet fabric of her swimming costume which had clung as stubbornly to her flesh as a parasitic limpet.

"Some things can never be unseen," Marigold whispered. "I think she must have prised her bulk into it with a shoehorn."

"Do spare me," I pleaded, hoping my wife didn't feel the need to elaborate.

When Violet Burke finally emerged from the toilet she had changed out of her aged skirted swimming costume into a shapeless brown splodged tent dress that could have passed muster as a cleaning overall.

"It wasn't easy washing my cossie out in that sink, some thieving idiot has only gone and knicked the plug," she complained.

"It's actually unusual for Greek wash basins to be fitted with plugs," I said, watching my mother lay her costume out on the bench seat to dry before stashing a packet of washing powder into her beach bag. I shared a bemused look with my wife when we realised my mother must have carted the bulky soap powder over from England since that particular brand wasn't available locally.

"I could have thrown that in the washing

machine for you when we got home," Marigold said.

"Do you really think that cossie would have survived for over half-a-century if I'd left it sitting around in corrosive salt water? You young'uns don't have a clue how to preserve things properly, everything is disposable these days."

"Well Victor has mastered the art of preserving things, you should see our vast collection of chutney," Marigold countered.

"Would you like a spray of my leave-in conditioner Vi, it will help to protect your hair against the drying effects of the sea water?" Adam offered.

"You're alright lad; my hair stayed nice and dry under my swimming cap. Now my stomach's fair growling, Benjamin pop down to the hold and fetch the picnic stuff, there's a love."

"A spot of light lunch is an excellent idea," I agreed, anticipating the flavoursome salad and dips which Marigold had prepared. If we waited a reasonable time after eating a light lunch it should be safe to venture back into the sea for another swim without risking vasoconstriction, leading to cramping and thus exacerbating the danger of drowning.

"I think you must have grabbed the wrong basket Benjamin, this isn't the lunch that I packed for us," Marigold said, confusion etched on her face as Benjamin unpacked the contents of the picnic basket. "Where is the big Tupperware dish of salad I prepared, and the containers of dips?"

"You can't expect growing lads to eat nothing but poxy salad, they aren't rabbits you know," my mother grumbled. "I realise you must be on one of them stupid fad diets Marigold, but you have to stop being so selfish and start feeding your husband up on something decent, it's not manly for him to keep eating all that green stuff."

"I am not on a diet..." Marigold protested.

"And I happen to love salad," I added.

"I don't know where you got the idea that I dictate what Victor eats, he does most of the cooking at home if you haven't noticed," Marigold snapped.

"Well Barry told me that you'd banned full English breakfasts, if I'd known that before flying out I'd have smuggled a nice bit of black pudding and some proper bangers over for Victor."

It was true that Marigold had been the one

to ban fry-ups, curtailing any enjoyment I might derive from a full English, but she only did it to prevent my arteries from getting all clogged up with fat and because she detests the lingering smell of fried food in the house. We had both agreed to adopt a healthier Greek diet once we'd settled in Meli and discovered the delicious delights of the local food. As for the accusation that Marigold was on some fad diet, it was patently absurd, as evidenced by the amount of sweet treats Marigold wantonly indulged in. She was particularly pleased that I didn't share her addiction to pistachio *halva* since she could selfishly gorge on it without feeling obliged to share it.

Before I had chance to voice my thoughts, my mother was back on her high-horse, insisting, "You could at least see what I've made you before you start complaining. It's a proper treat, though now I've opened the tins I'll have to shell out for a new wedding present for Barry and that bride of his."

Even though it may have been the polite thing to do the four of us failed to plaster fake expressions of delight on our faces when Violet Burke revealed an enormous stack of sorry looking Spam sandwiches. The unappetising things were crafted from the sliced bread stocked in the village store, the unpalatably thick dry stuff that was only fit for toasties.

"I thought you could do with a bit of good British food so I knocked up some Spam sarnies with a nice bit of salad cream."

"Spam isn't even British," I pointed out, unable to resist adding sarcastically, "The word is an acronym for Special Processed American Meat."

"I can't believe you took the liberty of substituting the lunch I prepared with that, I can't abide Spam," Marigold said crossly.

"I must confess I've never tried it, but here goes," Benjamin said, bravely taking a substantial bite from a Spam sandwich in solidarity with his granny.

Before Benjamin could pass judgement Vasos stumbled down the stairs from the wheelhouse, proclaiming *"peinao,"* meaning he was hungry.

"Para ena santouits," I said, inviting him to help himself to a sandwich. I was curious how Vasos would react to eating foreign food, but as unappetising as Violet Burke's picnic appeared the sandwiches were certainly an improvement on mouldering pie crusts. Chomping down on a

sandwich with all the enthusiasm of a starving man, Vasos suddenly became aware of my mother's presence, immediately claiming the seat next to her and spluttering through a mouthful of Spammy bread, "hello, hello, good, yes."

"Well it's good to see that someone appreciates the effort I went to," Violet Burke smirked, pressing another sandwich on the irrepressible *Kapetanios*. "Marigold, seeing as how you sneer at those Fray Bentos in the kitchen cupboard I'll do you a favour and take them off your hands. I have to come up with a new wedding gift now I've wasted all that Spam on you ungrateful lot."

Attempting to pretend my chortle was a cough, I turned away. Whilst Cynthia might share the same disdain for my secret stash of Fray Bentos as Marigold did, I knew that whilst Barry shared his sister's antipathy to Spam he had a definite weakness for tinned pies.

Following their second dive the three French men were relaxing on deck as Vasos steered Pegasus to the final dive spot. I wandered over to join Adam who was deep in conversation with the divers, pleased that my son-in-law to be, if gay marriage was ever legalised, was happy to translate for my benefit. I was curious to learn more about the nature of their underwater scientific research without trying to fathom my way through Henri's malapropisms.

I was fascinated to hear that the French men were studying submarine natural water springs as a potential viable source of fresh water for the area which suffered from water shortages, a persistent affliction we were all too familiar with up in the mountain village of Meli. Many of the villages above the coast had their water supply diverted to the tourist centres during the summer to make up for the shortfall: perish the thought that any tourists may have to suffer the inconvenience of having no water, even if it left our taps to run dry. The French men lamented that the springs appeared to lie beneath a solid formation of limestone rock which may well make any ambition to plug into the source economically unviable. I reasoned that if anything came of their research it would be aeons before the Greek government did anything about it, considering the way that Greek bureaucracy moved at a veritable snail's pace.

With my curiosity satisfied I excused myself, noticing that Marigold and Benjamin appeared to be deep in private conversation. Not wishing to interrupt their mother and son time I wondered if this could be my chance to speak privately with my own mother and raise the subject of my paternity. Presuming since Violet Burke was nowhere in sight that she was once again closeted in the toilet, I headed instead to the wheelhouse for a chat with Vasos who had definitely perked up after his impromptu lunch. It appeared that Spam sandwiches proved to be a remarkably effectual, if somewhat surprising, hangover cure.

I was taken aback to discover Violet Burke in the wheelhouse with Vasos, busily restoring order to the space. Throwing the accumulated rubbish into a bin bag she kept up a running commentary on the merits of cleanliness, Vasos nodding along even though he couldn't understand a word that she said.

"I don't know how you can find anything in such filth, here let me give those binoculars a wipe, they're all greasy," my mother chuntered.

"Good yes," Vasos responded, a beaming smile on his face. Spotting my presence Vasos threw an arm around Violet Burke's shoulder, saying, *"Victor, den mou eipes oti i matera sou itan toso omorfi."*

Staring at the captain I attempted to detect a trace of sarcasm in his words that I had never told him that my mother was so beautiful, but Vasos appeared to be genuine and free of guile.

"This towel is rancid, it needs a good boil wash," my mother continued, holding the offensive rag at arm's length.

"Towel, yes good," Vasos beamed.

"What are you like? The towel isn't good, it stinks," my mother said.

"Stinks," Vasos repeated, rolling the novel word around on his tongue. "Stinks beautiful. Stinks." Noting the captain appeared to have taken rather a liking to this new word I imagined how it would be received if he added it to his nine strong repertoire of English vocabulary and tested it out on his tourist charges.

My mother tipped the contents of a water bottle onto an old rag which she used to vigorously wipe the window overlooking the upper deck, releasing a strong smell of anise. I was quite surprised that ouzo proved to be such an effective glass cleaner, though a tad more pricey than tackling glass with vinegar and an old newspaper. Violet Burke continued her monologue as she scrubbed, Vasos nodding along and grinning, the pair of them at ease in one another's company even though neither of them could understand the other. Their easy companionship reminded me of the way that Violet Burke and Kyria Maria enjoyed each other's company over a shared cup of tea, forging a friendship despite the language barrier.

I decided to leave them to it and take a turn around the deck. As I stepped out of the wheelhouse my mother called out to me, "That Cynthia wants her head examining."

"How so?"

"To let a fine fellow like the captain slip through her fingers. I mean, don't get me wrong, Barry's a nice enough lad, but he doesn't come with his own yacht like this chap."

Chapter 16

Victor Pens his Speech

E ven though I had the best part of a free day to be getting on with penning my best man's speech for the next day, it was proving to be no simple task. Apart from the cats, I had the house to myself; it was lovely and quiet, Benjamin and Adam having driven up to town in the Punto to buy flowers to adorn the wedding venue. When I had suggested to Marigold that instead of tagging along with the boys we give them some alone time, she had interpreted this as a devious plot on my part to stick her with the task of entertaining my mother whilst I locked myself in my office to perfect my prose.

Even though I insisted her conspiracy theory was patently nonsense, my wife flounced off to Doreen's house for morning coffee. Marigold's accusations of my plotting were proved to be nothing but the product of her heated imagination when Violet Burke, well-oiled with our best extra virgin, retired to a sun lounger in the garden to work on her tan, demonstrating she was perfectly capable of making her own entertainment. Whilst her solitary sun worshipping presented the perfect opportunity for a private chat about my paternity, the clock was ticking and the speech wouldn't write itself. I reasoned that there was still plenty of opportunity to talk to my mother since she would be hogging our guest bedroom room for the next eleven nights.

Staring at the scrumpled pages of rejected words littering my office floor, the full enormity of the task hit me as it became clear such an important speech could be a potential minefield. Wishing I had heeded Marigold's sound advice to not leave it until the last minute I decided to Google some tips on composing a best man's speech, only to discover that the online advice presented a whole host of new challenges. General pointers suggested peppering the speech with humour and making a few ribald jokes at the groom's expense. However in light of Cynthia's rather obvious jealous streak I decided it was prudent to omit any mention of Barry's exes, even though they hadn't been particularly thick on the ground, to avoid unleashing Cynthia's green eyed inner monster.

Further useless online advice suggested including a few gay jokes and casual references to the best man being rather smitten with the groom. Whilst I regard Barry as not only an all-round excellent fellow but indeed a blood brother, I can't see him being comfortable with quips about my finding him attractive, nor do I wish to put such risible ideas into Cynthia's head. I considered there was nothing funny in incorporating gay jokes into my speech since they may only serve to remind Benjamin and Adam that they don't have the legal right to their own marriage celebration. Wondering who came up with such nonsensical drivel I turned the computer off in frustration and adjourned to the kitchen to compose a suitable speech, preferring to rely on my own common sense.

As I brewed some fresh coffee it struck me that raising a glass to absent friends was the usual order of business, but a toast to the missing Trouts might set Cynthia off by reminding her that her mother had been forcibly ejected from the flight to Greece. Surely the woman could have at least made the effort to sign up for a 'Fear of Flying' programme rather than letting her daughter down so publicly. The whole sorry business of the Trouts absence reminded me that I must include a special toast to Nikos for nobly stepping into the breach to give Cynthia away.

Recalling tedious wedding speeches that I had been forced to sit through over the years I remembered that it was rather the done thing to reference the bride's beauty and to compliment the stunning bridesmaids. I guessed that a few sentences about how glossy Cynthia's brunette hair is would cover the obligatory beautiful bride spiel; if she lifted the bridal veil by the time I delivered my speech then the guests could form their own opinion without any need for me to go over the top with false flattery. Thoughts of the veil reminded me to jot down a few words to thank Kyria Maria for coming to the rescue with the loan of the antique mantilla she had worn so many moons ago at her own wedding. I realised I could dispense with all standard references to stunning bridesmaids since Cynthia didn't have any lined up, unless she managed to sneak her vile mutant cat into the service. Thinking of Kouneli, I made a mental note to ask Guzim if I could lock the foul creature in his shed the next day, just in case Cynthia attempted to drag the repulsive feline into the mix.

Sitting at the kitchen table I penned a few words extolling Barry as an excellent brother-in-law, in addition to his being a staunch and loyal friend, and a wonderful new addition to the village. Reading over the words I had finally committed to paper, a sudden alarming thought struck me. Many of the guests would be forced to sit through my speech without actually understanding a word of English; they were bound to be bored witless. I considered dropping some pertinent Greek words into my speech, but that would only serve to confuse any English guests who didn't speak Greek.

The obvious solution was to give one speech in English followed by a second one in Greek, but the very thought of composing a speech in

Greek that had any hope of being even remotely grammatically correct left me overwhelmed. I considered rounding off my English speech with a simple Greek sentence thanking the Greek contingent for attending, but then I remembered how that had turned out the last time I'd tried it at the traditional house blessing ceremony. A wave of embarrassment coursed through me as I recalled thanking Papas Andreas for the honour of giving our house diarrhoea in carefully memorised and enunciated Greek. Deciding to take the easy way out I gave Spiros a call, asking him if he would be willing to stand beside me and translate my English speech into Greek, line by line.

Fortunately Spiros, as obliging as ever, agreed, with the proviso that I didn't drone on for too long in my apparently habitual style. I would have taken offence at his implication that I can be a tad boringly long-winded, but I was too desperate for his help. With that worry out of the way I continued to work on my speech until I was interrupted by Violet Burke barging into the kitchen to make a pot of tea.

"Maria from next door has popped round for a cuppa, she won't know what's hit her when she tastes proper PG Tips instead of that foul brew with twigs floating in it."

"Tsai tou vounou may have the odd twig in it but at least it is caffeine free. Anyway, where have you put Maria?" I asked, hoping my elderly neighbour wasn't about to put in an appearance in the kitchen. Kyria Maria had a tendency to stick her fingers in any foreign foodstuffs she considered curiosities, rendering them only fit for the bin after her unhygienic poking. Whilst any tinned stuff was safe from her mitts, she seemed to be under the impression that anything with a screw top was ripe for a thorough mauling. Marigold was still vexed that she'd been forced to bin a jar of stem ginger after Maria explored the contents with grubby fingers, not a thought to washing her hands after petting Guzim's tame rabbit.

"She's down in the garden. I'll chuck a couple of Warrington eggs on the tea tray; it's about time for elevenses…"

"Mother it's barely gone ten," I pointed out.

"But there's the time difference to consider."

"It's only eight in the morning back in Warrington."

"You always have to have the last word, that's something I've noticed about you Victor."

"I can't possibly imagine where I get it from."

"There you go again, having to have the last word," she retorted.

"Let me carry the tray outside for you," I offered. My motive wasn't entirely altruistic; I was itching to see Kyria Maria's expression when she encountered a Warrington egg, recalling from my mother's previous visit that this particular northern delicacy comprised a pickled Scotch egg coated in black pudding and batter before being deep fried. It appeared that on this occasion Violet Burke had filled her suitcase with eggs which she had deep fried in advance. Surely by now the battered Warrington delicacies must have turned decidedly soggy.

I hoped that Kyria Maria had a strong stomach since the Warrington eggs had been nowhere near the refrigerator since landing in Greece. On the other hand, I reflected, a dodgy stomach may prevent Kyria Maria from turning up at the wedding reception and guzzling any canapés that took her fancy, before dumping anything that didn't appeal back on the platter after a good fingering. My thoughts reminded me that I needed to have a word with Nikos to ensure he was planning to cater enough canapés for any guests who turned up unexpectedly. Bumping into Giannis the other day had demonstrated that we needed to be prepared to feed any random arrivals who weren't included on the official guest list.

Clad in her usual black widow's weeds, Kyria Maria perched primly on the edge of a sun lounger, her back ramrod straight, mirroring the upright position she favoured when sitting in her own garden on a hard backed kitchen chair. I could tell from her posture that she was uncomfortable with the notion of idly lying around on a sun lounger.

"*Ta kotopoula einai oraia kai lipara,*" Kyria Maria said, keenly observing my brood of chickens.

"What's she saying?" my mother demanded.

"She said that the chickens look nice and fat."

"I told you they'd make a lovely roast dinner," my mother gloated.

"*Ti eipe?*" Maria asked.

"*Tipota,*" I lied, preferring to say that Vi had said nothing rather than be roped into translating their every inane utterance.

"*Ti einai afto?*" Maria asked, looking at the deep fried offerings with suspicion.

"What's she saying?" my mother demanded.

"She's asking what those are," I replied before switching to Greek and telling Maria *"einai avga Warrington."*

"Ti?" Maria fired back.

"Tell her this is a proper English cuppa, not any of that twig muck," my mother ordered.

"Ti eipe?" Maria repeated, her frustration visibly rising as she once again asked what my mother was saying.

Ignoring Maria's question I said "I must get back and finish my speech for tomorrow," before beating a hasty retreat. Legging it up the stairs I could hear my mother telling Kyria Maria to get some proper English tea inside her, relieved that I had a good excuse to escape translation duties. The two old dears could talk at one other companionably I reasoned. Their conversation was hardly likely to be so earth shattering that a spot of translation would make it more exciting.

I had just penned a particularly witty line in my speech when I was once again disturbed, this time by Milton, our impoverished genteel British neighbour.

"Morning old chap, hope this isn't an inconvenient time. I was at a bit of a loose end since Edna is off having morning coffee with Doreen and your wife. Girls only don't you know, us chaps aren't welcome."

I peered past Milton to make sure he was alone. I was in no mood for Doreen's dull as ditch water husband Norman to be tagging along behind Milton.

"I can spare five minutes Milton," I said, putting the kettle on. "But then I really have to be getting on with my speech for the wedding tomorrow. It wouldn't do to be caught out with a blank piece of paper."

"I can give you a few pointers if you like old chap," Milton offered. "You just need plenty of guff about how beautiful the bride is. Exaggerate if necessary about the bridesmaids being stunning, no one expects it to be true. No matter how pretty they are they usually end up looking like the dog's breakfast in some ghastly frock they wouldn't be seen dead in, but for the bride insisting they wear it. Brides usually demand something dreary and puffy because they hate to be outdone on their big day, don't you know. Throw in a couple of gags about how you've always quite fancied the groom, that's always good for a laugh. A bit of gay humour is usually expected at that sort of shindig."

"I'll certainly bear that in mind," I said politely, wondering if Milton held down a secret job writing complete twaddle on internet advice sites since his recommendations certainly mirrored the baloney I'd come across earlier. "It's been very kind of you to give Cynthia a bed; we've got a full house here with my family over from England."

"Think nothing of it old chap, it's been our pleasure to have a bit of company beside the cats. Must say I'm looking forward to tomorrow, it will be the first Greek wedding we've been to. Cynthia mentioned you were splurging on canapés, can't say I've ever come across a Greek canapé before, should be interesting to see what they come up with."

"Well it's not really a Greek wedding as such. They couldn't have an Orthodox Church wedding without converting. The ceremony in the *Dimarcheio* is probably equivalent to a registry office service back in England."

"Ah, but they don't go in for all that tooting back in England."

"Tooting?" I queried.

"With the car horns. Everyone drives in convoy from the service to the reception without taking their hands off the horn. Frightful din I thought the first time I heard it, until I found out what it was all about."

"That sounds a tad ear-splitting, surely it breaks some local regulation against noise pollution," I said, inwardly cringing at the thought of the newlyweds being serenaded with a good forty minutes' drive worth of cacophonic hooting. It wouldn't do to have everyone crying off the reception early, complaining they'd been struck down with a mass migraine.

"It's the local tradition old chap. I say this is good stuff, don't say you've managed to get your hands on some PG Tips?"

I cast my mind back to the wedding of Eleni and Kostis. They had married in the church in Meli and I hadn't associated the blasting of car horns with any tradition since the drive to the reception had taken less than a minute. I had presumed the honking had merely been a sign of impatience by ravenous Greeks eager to get stuck into the wedding feast.

Moving over to the kitchen table I shuffled around a few of the papers, hoping that Milton would take the hint that I needed to get on with the important business of speech writing. Fortunately Milton proved quick on the uptake.

"Well I won't keep you old chap, excellent cuppa. Darn, I almost forgot why I dropped in; I wonder if you'd mind casting your eye over this letter Edna's typed up, it's a query letter to attach to 'Delicious Desire' when I send it off to publishers of erotica. I took your advice old chap and researched some reputable companies that don't charge a dime."

"If you don't mind leaving it with me Milton I'll be happy to take a look at the letter once the wedding is out of the way," I said, glancing at it briefly and noting it was only a couple of pages containing a bare, but rather explicit, synopsis of his book.

"Excellent, excellent, I'll leave it in your capable hands then," Milton said gratefully as I popped his letter down on the kitchen table.

"Put the kettle on for another pot of tea Victor, I'm just going to dig some more Warrington eggs out of my suitcase; Maria can't get enough of them," my mother barked from the doorway. Presuming that my mother was deluding herself I hoped that my elderly Greek neighbour wasn't surreptitiously feeding the eggs to my chickens. Before I could put that point to my mother she had disappeared, scuttling off to raid her suitcase. Turning my attention back to

Milton I noticed he was clutching hold of the kitchen table as though to hold himself up, his ashen face a pale mask of its former self.

"Are you okay Milton, you look a tad peaky?" I asked, worried he was about to keel over.

"I just came over a bit faint, I couldn't trouble you for a glass of water old chap," Milton replied, his voice a weak tremor of its usual assured timbre.

"Perhaps you could do with a breath of fresh air," I suggested. Taking his arm I led him out to the balcony and guided him into a chair, before rushing back inside for a glass of water. Thinking he was in no fit shape to be introduced to my mother I stuck my head around the spare room door to tell her I'd bring the tea down to her and Maria.

"Make sure you don't scrimp on the tea bags, one each and one for the pot," my mother instructed.

Even after downing his glass of water Milton still looked like death warmed up. Worst case scenarios raced through my mind; perhaps Milton was stricken with a contagious illness he may well have passed onto Cynthia. Recalling that Cynthia had been feeling off colour all week

I felt a wave of shame for so readily dismissing her queasiness as a hangover without interrogating her on the state of her general health, though Marigold had brushed it off as nothing more than pre-wedding nerves. Still it would be a disaster if Milton had indeed passed something nasty onto Cynthia and she became too indisposed to go through with the wedding; after all I had already shelled out the readies for the canapés and put so much effort into my speech.

"Try putting your head between your knees," I advised Milton.

"No need, the air and water have revived me old chap. I'd best be getting out of your way, know what a busy chap you are."

"Have another glass of water before you make tracks," I encouraged, thinking he still looked a shadow of his former self. As I topped up his glass it occurred to me that Milton may be feeling faint due to hunger. Speculating that he and Edna may be feeling the pinch and rationing their food intake, I wrapped up a spare lemon drizzle cake for their elevenses. After draining the second glass of water a touch of colour returned to Milton's face, but since he still looked a tad frail I insisted on walking him home, worried that if he fainted and fell over en-route it could play havoc with his new hip.

"Not a word about this to Edna, old chap, no point in worrying the old girl," Milton implored as we reached his gate.

"But surely it would be wise for her to be in the know if you are sick," I protested.

"Never felt better old chap, not a trace of sickness. I just had a bit of a shock that's all, a blast from the past that rather the knocked all the stuffing out of me."

"A blast from the past?" I repeated.

"Stupid of me really, but the old brain plays tricks when you get to my age. Mind you it's not the first that time that I've imagined seeing her; I haven't managed to shake off her image in sixty years…still I must need my head examining to imagine I saw Violet Bloom in your house, after all what on earth could she possibly be doing in this remote bit of Greece. Ignore me old chap, it's just that sometimes the slightest reminder triggers the past."

"Well if you're sure that you are okay," I muttered, hurrying away as quickly as my legs could carry me. As soon as I rounded the corner and was safely out of sight I sank onto the nearest wall, my equilibrium disturbed as I pondered the possible connection that may exist between Milton and Violet Burke, nee Blossom.

Chapter 17

A Naïve and Gullible Fool

I have no idea how long I avoided returning home, rooted to the wall deep in contemplation, trying to get my head around the notion that Milton not only knew my mother but had been clearly knocked for six by the merest glimpse of her. Confused thoughts flooded my mind as I gazed into the distance, oblivious to the natural beauty around me.

"Victor, what on earth has happened, your face is the very picture of doom? Don't tell me the wedding is off? I popped into the shop on my way home from Doreen's and saw you sitting there as I queued up to pay. You haven't moved a muscle since I first spotted you, something's clearly wrong Victor, tell me what it is."

Looking up I registered Marigold's presence, the concern in her voice bringing me out of my trance.

"You don't have any shopping," I numbly observed.

"Just some painkillers."

"Are you in pain?" I asked.

"I lost a filling biting into one of Doreen's flapjacks, it's agony, it's never been right since the first time the filling broke off on that dry cat food, " Marigold said taking my hand. "But never mind that now Victor, you are acting very strangely, do tell me what's the matter. Is the wedding off or is it something else?"

"Milton called round…"

"Did Cynthia send him because she has changed her mind? I'll never forgive her if she breaks Barry's heart and dumps him at the altar."

Not bothering to pedantically remind my wife that the wedding would not actually feature an altar to be left at, I assured her, "No, it is nothing like that, the wedding is still on. Milton came over all funny, shock would best describe it. Apparently he caught sight of my mother…"

"Well I can understand that she may come across as a bit scary, but she's not really that bad, at least in small doses. We've really been getting on quite well this visit…"

"Marigold, will you allow me to finish a sentence without interrupting?" Taking a deep breath I realised that I had been unnecessarily curt with my wife. "Sorry darling, I didn't mean to snap, but you did ask what was wrong. I walked Milton home because he was rather shaken up. I thought he was sick but then he said the strangest thing…"

"Go on," Marigold encouraged.

"He said he thought he saw Violet Bloom in the house. Of course he clearly saw her, but it was his reaction to it that was so odd, extreme in fact, I wouldn't have been surprised if he'd keeled over with a heart attack."

"That does sound like an extreme reaction. Did your mother react strangely too?"

"She didn't even notice him; you know how she bulldozes ahead with blinkers on," I said. "Milton told me that he had been unable to shake off her image for sixty years."

"He must have it bad if he could even recognise her after six decades, surely she must have changed."

"And another thing that was decidedly off, when I voiced my concern about the shock he was in, he begged me not to mention it to Edna."

"Oh I say, I think I know where you're heading with this Victor. Are you thinking they had some sort of romantic entanglement in the past, or even worse a sordid affair? Oh, we'll never live it down if your mother was the inspiration behind Milton's porn, and to think all this time we just assumed Edna was his muse."

"I never even gave that a thought Marigold. I was too busy wondering if Milton could possibly be my father."

"I think you're making rather a leap there Victor, you know Vi was pretty sure that Vic the soap salesman got her pregnant. We don't even know if your mother had any involvement with Milton. I think you're just clutching at straws because you hate the thought of your father being an army deserter, but does a pornographer really sound any better?"

"You know as well as I do that Milton pens erotica, not porn," I said defensively. "I can't imagine that Milton would have reacted in such a shocked manner if they were mere acquaintances, she obviously left a lasting impression on him."

"Well the best thing to do is head home and speak to your mother at once, don't beat about the bush. Just ask her straight how their paths crossed," Marigold advised.

"What would I do without you?" I asked.

"Well luckily you will never need to find out," she replied. As Marigold spoke I noticed the way she pressed her hand against her cheek, attempting to hide an involuntary stab of pain.

"Did you take a painkiller?" I asked.

"The shop only had *Depon*, I think I need something much stronger than paracetamol," Marigold sighed.

"You need a dentist, darling. You must get that filling sorted out before the wedding," I said firmly, knowing how even the thought of the dentist's chair filled Marigold with dread. "Come on, I'll make you an appointment as soon as we get home."

Relieved to see that Maria had left and that my mother was alone in the garden I squatted down beside her sun lounger. Attempting to broach the subject in a casual manner I said, "Mother, you didn't tell me you knew Milton."

"Can't say I know anyone called Milton. Is there any tea left in that pot?"

"Milton Hancock, he's our neighbour here in Meli, Cynthia is staying with him and his wife Edna until the wedding," I persisted.

"It doesn't ring a bell. Oh hang on, I do know an Edna, but we aren't on first name terms. Mrs Billings what comes in for her haddock every Friday is an Edna, horrible woman... we did used to be on first name terms until she disparaged my cod, but now we keep it more formal."

Obviously Mrs Billings wasn't Milton's Edna. "Do you remember meeting a Milton during the war?" I persisted.

"I can't say I do Victor and my mind's pretty sharp. Now give me a hand up off this lounger, I need the toilet."

Hauling my mother to her feet it was clear that she had no clue who Milton was. As always she appeared perfectly transparent, with no hint of attempting to dissemble.

With Violet Burke locked in the bathroom I relayed our conversation to Marigold. Knowing that it would prey obsessively on my mind unless I got to the bottom of things, Marigold encouraged me to call in on Milton.

"I'll come with you darling and keep Edna distracted so that you can speak privately with Milton. Come on, there's no time like the present."

True to her word Marigold deftly spirited Edna out to the garden with the lure of some cuttings from her potted plants which she insisted on helping Edna pot up right away. Alone with Milton in his sitting room, I didn't waste any time beating around the bush, asking him how he knew Violet Blossom without revealing that she was in fact my mother.

"I was intrigued by your reaction when you thought you'd seen someone from the past. Was it someone special to you?" I asked, hoping my face didn't give away my intense personal reasons for sticking my nose in.

"Special to me, but I daresay I was just one of hundreds of admirers…"

"And this was during the war?"

"Back in my RAF days, old chap. I was stationed at Bratton and the command needed a message taking over to the Yanks at Burtonwood. Harvey and I volunteered; we weren't going to pass up the chance for a night at the Casino Ballroom in Warrington, some sort of

Art Deco venue one wouldn't expect to find in the north. It had a fabulous reputation for hosting the hottest jazz musicians. You can imagine what a downer it was when we got to the Casino and were turned away at the door. Orders from above decreed that all service personnel were banned, a most deplorable decision."

I wished that Milton would get to the point since I was finding it difficult to feign interest in his convoluted account. My sole interest was in discovering his connection to my mother.

"We went to a popular pub instead, the Pelican. She caught my eye as soon as we walked in, a busty redhead with a shapely set of pins doing the jitterbug. She was the most striking creature I'd ever seen, not conventionally pretty but so distinctive that she took my breath away. With Harvey egging me on I eventually plucked up the nerve to buy her a rum and lime, and that's when she told me her name was Violet Blossom. I remember her lamenting the lack of nylons and what a nuisance it was to paint seams on her legs with gravy. One of the Yanks we'd run into at Burtonwood had a supply of nylons he was willing to trade. I told her I'd try to get hold of some and she agreed to meet me outside the Pelican the next evening. I couldn't believe my good fortune when she agreed."

Despite Violet Burke's denial of knowing Milton there appeared no doubt that it was indeed my mother that Milton had run into. Even if perchance there were two women who shared the name Violet Blossom, the chance of them both being busty redheads struck me as slim.

"I was a bag of nerves the next evening, sweaty palms and all that don't you know. She was so late arriving that I thought she'd stood me up, and then out of nowhere she was there. Her face lit up when I gave her the nylons, she was grateful to have then; and then she kissed me..."

It was clear that Milton, gazing into the distance, was lost in his memories of the past as he spoke. Hoping he wouldn't divulge any intimate details of what happened next, I nevertheless urged him to continue his story.

"She excused herself when we went inside, saying she was going to slip the nylons on in the ladies' room. I bought her a rum and lime while I waited at the bar, she was gone an absolute age. The next thing I knew Harvey rolled up and said we had orders to get back to Bratton at the double. I couldn't just leave and stand her up, but when I looked round to tell her I had to go I saw her dancing with another fellow, a Yank. The way they were holding each other was so intimate that I realised our date meant nothing to her...and it broke my heart. I couldn't face speaking to her so I just slipped out with Harvey."

"And did you ever see her again?"

"No, but I never shook her image. It can be months and then something reminds me of her and it takes me right back to 1943 and the Pelican."

I'm afraid to say that Milton's tale of heartbreak left me decidedly unmoved. It was obviously a case of unrequited love from a naïve and gullible fool who had jumped to the conclusion that their meeting was a date when it was clearly nothing more than an exchange of bartered goods, a kiss in return for a pair of nylons. To carry an image of a woman who had clearly worked her charms in order to get her pins into a pair of stockings rather exposed Milton as an inexperienced dewy-eyed sap. My overriding feeling was one of relief that my mother's looseness with her favours in return for the nylons, at least with Milton, had been limited to a kiss.

Nevertheless I was left with a dilemma. Although Milton had obviously made no impression at all on Violet Burke she had clearly left an abiding impression on him, and they would come face to face the next day at the wedding. The only decent thing to do was prepare Milton by telling him that the woman he'd met in the Pelican more than sixty years ago was in fact my mother. It wouldn't do to let him walk into the lion's den unprepared and make a fool of himself in front of Edna by confessing his unrequited love to my mother. Although I considered that carrying a six decade long torch for a woman he'd only met briefly made Milton a lovesick fool, I nevertheless realised I must burst his bubble with tact.

"Milton you need to know that Violet Blossom is my mother, though she's Violet Burke now. She's staying with us at the moment and she will be at Barry's wedding tomorrow."

"That's a bit of a rum do old chap. Do you suppose it's too early for a whiskey? Oh blast it, pour me one anyway, it's all a bit of a shock."

Chapter 18

A Rabies Shot

Really, you shouldn't have Vi, you're on your holidays," Marigold said, practically asphyxiating with me an aerosol air-freshener and flagrantly rolling her eyes as my mother dished up the lunch she had prepared whilst we had been over at Milton's place.

"Well I knew that if I left it up to you there'd be nothing but oily salad. Tuck in Victor, you won't get better than my Spam fritters and mash."

"I couldn't eat a thing with this tooth," Marigold said, sinking into a chair, her genuine wince of pain masking her disgust for the unappetising battered Spam.

"More likely you've got no appetite from filling your face with lemon drizzle. There was a full one in the cake tin this morning and now the whole thing has been guzzled."

"I gave the cake to Milton to take home in case their dire financial situation has left them short on food again," I explained.

"Really Vi, I wish you'd think before throwing out wild accusations," Marigold complained. "Yesterday you were convinced I was on a fad diet and now you have me down as a secret binge eater."

"It sounds as though you've got yourself one of them fashionable eating disorders," Violet Burke accused, bulldozing ahead with her opinion. "Have some mash at least, you needn't worry it will do more damage to your tooth, I got all the lumps out."

Toying with my fritter I said, "Mother, remember I asked you earlier if you knew Milton?"

"I'm not senile yet. It's hardly an hour since I told you I don't know anyone called Milton."

"Well it turns out that he remembers meeting you during the war. You met up at the Pelican Pub…"

"The Pelican, I don't recall," my mother interrupted. "Hang on you're thinking of the Dirty Bird, that's what us locals called it. It got quite popular with the Yanks once servicemen were banned from the Ballroom."

"What on earth did they do get banned?" Marigold asked.

"Nothing, the club didn't ban them, it was the higher-ups. There were some GIs from the south that objected to black soldiers being allowed in, but the club wouldn't back down and ban them. It was a disgrace it was, they were happy enough to have black musicians playing while they danced, but they refused to socialise in the same place. I met Ulysses in the Ballroom." My mother smiled fondly, taking her own trip down memory lane.

"I remember you mentioning Ulysses before; he was your black beau from Mississippi."

"That's right, I couldn't give tuppence for what people thought. I had hopes of marrying him until you came out white."

That would be before I was coated in coal dust from the filthy receptacle I'd been dumped in, I reflected.

"What has any of this got to do with Milton?" Marigold asked.

"I'm just getting to that," I said, recounting the tale that Milton had told me earlier.

"Are you saying there's some poor sap out there who I gave a kiss to in exchange for some nylons, and he's been carrying a torch for sixty years?"

"Perhaps seeing Milton at the wedding tomorrow will jog your memory. You clearly left a lasting impression Mother."

"Well I was no shrinking Violet, in spite of my name. I'm still none the wiser who this Milton fellow is. We had to kiss a lot of frogs back then to keep up with the fashions. I hope he's not going to go and make a fool of himself at the wedding; I'm past all that flirting malarkey now."

"Milton will be at the wedding, but as he will be with his wife Edna I am sure that he won't subject you to any unwanted advances."

"Thank goodness for that because I swore off men after Arthur."

Meeting my wife's eyes we shared one of those moments where our thoughts meshed in perfect sync; we were both willing the other not to encourage my mother by asking who Arthur was. Having only just weathered the shock of Milton's connection to Violet Burke, any other information at this point would be an overload my system couldn't cope with. Any further questions regarding my paternity would have to be put on hold until the wedding was out of the way.

As Marigold's fingers dug into my right thigh with bruise inducing pressure I reflected that my decision to make a wardrobe adjustment several years back, switching from swimming trunks to swim shorts, was a fortuitous one. The bruises I could feel forming were unlikely to fade anytime soon, but at least my swim shorts would provide suitable cover on my next public dip, concealing the signs that I had been man-handled. Driving to the dentist's office Marigold's fear was palpable, trepidation oozing from her in waves. Although not nervous by nature beyond her fear of creepy-crawlies sneaking indoors, Marigold was a gibbering wreck when it came to the dentist. To her credit she'd had no wish to pass on her irrational fear to Benjamin during his formative years, thus I had been charged with taking our son for his childhood check-ups. The arrangement was a re-sounding success; Benjamin has lovely teeth and didn't inherit his mother's fear of the dentist.

Marigold's dental appointment was the first time either of us had needed personal medical attention since moving to Greece. Naturally my first port of call in seeking a recommendation for a dentist was Spiros. Although he knew several orthodontists he couldn't offer a personal recommendation since he hadn't had his teeth checked in over two decades, something I ought to have guessed by the shocking state of his teeth. Vangelis proved equally useless, freely admitting that he would rather resort to pulling out any tooth of his that rotted with a pair of pliers from his tool box, than subject himself to the torture of the dentist's chair.

Vangelis did offer the name of Athena's dentist since his wife, being less squeamish than he, didn't share his dentophobia. However the practice Athena frequented was in town and Marigold knew that her nerves would never survive the three-hour round trip; she dismissed out of hand my suggestion of swallowing a generous dose of cat sedatives to calm her nerves for the journey. Fortunately a call to Cynthia elicited the name of a dentist on the coast where she went for regular check-ups, never once neglecting her six month appointments.

When I'd phoned and secured an emergency appointment for six o'clock that afternoon Marigold had bravely overcome her reservations, acknowledging, "Cynthia does have lovely teeth." I had to agree that Cynthia's gnashers were almost as glossy as her hair.

As we waited for the dentist to admit us I advised, "Take a deep breath," flexing the fingers that Marigold had squeezed the life out of during our short walk from the car. The door was flung open by a large, solidly built woman in surgical gloves who silently ushered us in, directing us up a staircase to an empty waiting room.

"Sit, sit," she instructed in English before heading back into the treatment room. The open door presented a clear view of the reclining legs of the patient currently receiving treatment, though we were spared the sight of anything above his belt. The open door did nothing to dull the sound of the dental drill. Marigold, her nerves already on edge, almost jumped out of her skin when the buzzer sounded. Abandoning her patient the dentist stalked past us in response to the buzzer, barking *"min fovitheite,"* meaning don't be frightened, her words carrying the authority of an order rather than reassurance. Amazingly Marigold stopped shaking, clearly daunted by the formidable woman.

The dentist returned deep in conversation with a young Greek man clutching his jaw, wearing a buttoned down white shirt over a vest, paired with black trousers, clearly the distinctive garb of a restaurant waiter. After listening to his pleas that he had to rush back to work quickly the dentist assured the new arrival that he could jump the queue and go next, *"prin apo ton tourista."* I bridled on Marigold's behalf that she had been so readily dismissed as a tourist, recalling that I had made the appointment in my best telephone Greek. Even though sitting around waiting whilst the waiter was prodded and poked would play havoc with Marigold's nerves, she exhaled in relief to have been granted a temporary reprieve.

The silence of the waiting room was only disturbed by the sound of the dental drill. My reassuring quip that the absence of screams was a good sign did little to dispel the tension. When the current patient trooped out a plume of smoke wafted in from the treatment room, leading me to suspect that the dentist was sneaking a crafty cigarette between patients. I began to doubt Cynthia's judgement when the dentist appeared in the doorway, a cigarette clamped between her surgically gloved fingers as she called the waiter inside. Fortunately Marigold didn't notice, too intent on practicing some deep breathing exercises with her eyes closed. Realising that voicing my concerns about surgical glove hygiene would do little to alleviate Marigold's shredded nerves, I sensibly kept schtum, clueless where we could find an alternative orthodontist at short notice.

The dentist kept up a one-sided conversation with the waiter who was presumably unable to respond. I admit to shamelessly eavesdropping, pleased to be able to decipher much of the dentist's inane line of chatter only punctuated with the odd ouch from the waiter. Stifled groans of pain from the waiter filtered into Marigold's conscious but I reassured her that everything would be fine, reminding her that she'd be able to flash her pearly whites painlessly for the wedding photographs once she overcame the dental hurdle.

Still clutching his jaw, the waiter emerged from the inner sanctum and the dentist called

Marigold in. Since my wife was clearly too stressed to cope with attempting to converse in Greek I accompanied her, replying to the dentist's questioningly raised eyebrow by saying "*tha metafraso*": I will translate.

"*Pes mou,*" the dentist said, tell me. Having copied the relevant words from the dictionary that I needed to say 'she is in a lot of pain after losing her filling,' I was prepared for this question. Enunciating clearly I said, "*Auto einai se poly pono meta tin apoleia tis ripsimo.*"

"*Ripsimo,*" the dentist repeated, poking inside her left earhole with a surgically gloved finger. "*Ti rispsimo?*"

Frantically thumbing through my pocket English to Greek dictionary I discovered to my mortification that I had just informed the dentist that my wife had lost a fling rather than a filling. I quickly corrected myself, substituting the word *ripsimo* with *plirosi.*

"*Anoixe,*" the dentist barked at Marigold, instructing her to open her mouth. Whilst Marigold cowered with her mouth agape, the dentist stripped off the contaminated with tobacco and earwax surgical gloves, rolling a fresh pair over her fingers. I shuddered inwardly at her lax attention to hygiene, noticing her failure to sanitise her hands. Knowing that my wife wouldn't thank me if launched into a lecture on optimum sterile practices and got us kicked out, I let the dentist's insanitary habit slide; in truth I did find the dentist a tad intimidating. Moving closer I reached over to put a reassuring hand on Marigold's shoulder, only to have the dentist snap *"fyge"* at me, meaning get away. As the dentist prodded around inside Marigold's mouth with a few fearsome looking instruments, Marigold attempted to speak. Fortunately I am well versed in interpreting my wife's blathering and understood she was requesting an injection.

"Thelei ena emvolio," I said on Marigold's behalf.

Pausing her prodding the dentist responded *"Yiate, pire lyssa?"*

I racked my brain to come up with the English translation of *lyssa*, knowing that it was a word I had come across very recently. As it suddenly dawned on me that the word had cropped up during a discussion with Panos about the chances of wild dogs being infected with rabies, I was flummoxed. Was the dentist seriously asking me if my wife had rabies?

I felt rather foolish when the dentist suddenly switched to English, saying "you tell me the woman want the *embolio*."

"Yes, so that she doesn't feel any pain."

"*Embolio* is the vaccination."

"I meant injection."

"You mean *enesi*. Why he want the *enesi*? It is not the necessary, I only to drill, all finish in the ten minutes. The last patient not need it."

"Please give her an injection, she's very nervous," I pleaded.

"Why? It will make the mouth numb? Better to feel if I work on the right tooth…"

"It's the tooth with the hole where the filling fell out," I explained. "Please inject her."

"You think I am the butcher? If the woman want numb I inject her even though not the necessary," the dentist shouted in exasperation, wielding the largest anaesthesia needle I had ever encountered.

Thirty minutes later Marigold was mainlining brandy through a straw in the nearest bar, attempting to disguise the dribble escaping from her puffed up mouth. Since she was incapable of making a coherent sound she wrote a note telling me to telephone Barry on the mobile and demand that he give Cynthia a piece of her mind for recommending such a sadistic dentist.

I have to say that I couldn't fault Barry's logic when he reported that Cynthia had only good things to say about the dentist, but then again she had only ever been there for her regular six month check-ups. Cynthia looked after her teeth so well that she hadn't needed any actual dental treatment whilst living in Greece.

Chapter 19

Back to his Old Tricks

N o one else up yet Victor?" Barry called over from the sofa, stretching and yawning as he dragged himself up.

"When's the last time you saw Marigold up with the lark?"

"Fair point," Barry laughed. "What about the rest of them?"

"I took my mother a cuppa in bed and per-suaded her to have a bit of a lie-in as it's sure to be a late night. Benjamin and Adam are already up and off. One of Spiros' contacts at the *Di-*

marcheio gave the go-ahead for the boys to slip in as soon as it opens and festoon the room with flowers. They'll be back in plenty of time to change into their wedding suits so you might want to claim first dibs on the shower," I advised. "It's a pity the boys could only get their hands on plastic blooms for décor but we can pick something fresh from the garden for our boutonnieres. I'm sure Marigold won't mind us raiding her flowering pot plants in the circumstances."

"Cynthia is going to be pretty miffed if she has to carry a plastic bouquet," Barry said, looking worried.

"It's all in hand; Athena is arranging a fresh bridal posy. Her green fingers have quite the reputation amongst the ladies that beautify the cemetery," I reassured Barry. "I've been taking advantage of the peace and quiet to go through the running order of the day. Events like this need organising with military precision, I need to put a tick against everything on the list."

"You're certainly the man for the job, Victor. I trust you implicitly to ensure everything runs smoothly."

"Don't worry Barry, you're in more than capable hands. My organisational skills prevented half the population of Manchester from coming down with mass food poisoning during my time at the Foods Standard Agency."

"I remember how you identified that plastic wrapped salad as being the toxic culprit in that mysterious outbreak of... what was it again Victor?"

"Cyclosporiasis, a tricky one to spot, it's caused by eating food contaminated with the cylospora parasite."

"It sounds nasty; at least all our salad stuff comes out of your garden now. What time do we need to be ready?"

"Well, the service is scheduled to take place at twelve noon sharp at the *Dimarcheio* so the two of us must be in place no later than eleven thirty. We really need to be leaving Meli no later than ten thirty; we need to allow for goats obstructing the road or tourists dawdling at twenty kilometres an hour."

"I can't believe I'm really getting married today, I'm a lucky man to have won Cynthia's heart."

"Nervous at all?" I asked.

"I might need an extra swipe with the roll-on deodorant," Barry admitted.

"I just hope that the two of you will be as

happy as Marigold and I have been," I said, trying to recall if I had added that little gem to my best man's speech, regretting that I hadn't had time to memorise it. "Did you check the oil and water in Cynthia's car? We can't afford to break down en-route to the wedding."

Since Meli lacked a limousine service we were making use of our available vehicles rather than arriving in extravagant style. Barry and I would drive to the *Dimarcheio* in Cynthia's old banger, leaving the Punto for Marigold, my mother and the boys. The bride was being driven down by Nikos who was giving her away, and the guests that were attending the service were responsible for making their own way there. I wasn't quite clear how many planned to attend the actual service since some of the villagers weren't up for the forty minute journey, but they promised to join the marriage celebrations in the village taverna.

Worried that Nikos had prepared enough canapés to feed any unexpected arrivals I had called into the taverna the previous evening, relieved when Nikos assured me that the canapés were big enough for everyone; an odd choice of phrase to be sure, but definitely reassuring. I was touched when he told me that some of the ladies in the village had volunteered to give Dina a hand preparing the wedding feast. I really liked the way everyone mustered together in village solidarity.

"You won't forget to collect Harold's house keys," Barry reminded me.

"You can count on me," I hastily assured my brother-in-law. In truth my key collecting duties had completely slipped my mind. I didn't relish the prospect of liaising with Harold, though with any luck it would prove to be my final encounter with the boorish oaf. I made a mental note to call by to collect the keys after breakfast, before returning home to change. The clear blue skies promised the day would be another scorcher and I didn't want to be caught out in a heat wave sweating into my wedding finery.

"I must go and wake Marigold with a coffee," I said. "She won't want to be late for her hair appointment in Athena's kitchen; Marigold, Cynthia and my mother are all having their hair done together."

"I hope Athena doesn't go overboard with the hair spray, I like Cynthia's hair all natural and glossy," Barry said, a lovesick smile on his face. "Has Marigold recovered from her ordeal at the dentist yet?"

"She was fine once her puffiness went down and she said that the tooth is as good as new. It put a bit of a dent in my credit card, I've a feeling that the dentist charged extra for the injection..."

"You should have tried a bit of bartering, a free filling for a day trip on Pegasus perhaps," Barry laughed.

"I'd rather pay the full price than spend a day in the company of that insanitary chain-smoking sadist," I retorted, taking a coffee through to the bedroom. I had only just roused Marigold when Barry tapped on the door, telling me that Guzim was on the doorstep requesting my presence. I could do without the interruption; I had enough on my plate with the wedding arrangements to oversee without dealing with any of Guzim's nonsense. Reflecting that it may be a chicken emergency I attempted to hide my annoyance as I greeted the Albanian shed dweller hovering in my doorway.

Flashing me a toothless grin Guzim launched into a fast-paced indecipherable whine whilst unfurling the piece of tattered checkered cloth he was clutching. Flapping the fabric in my face unleashed the fetid stench of chicken droppings clinging to what turned out to be a shabby shirt that looked suspiciously like a bring-and-buy reject. Guzim continued apace in a wielding tone.

Struggling to comprehend what he was chuntering on about, I managed to make out the odd word, recognising *'poukamiso'* shirt, *'chrimata'* money, and *'Alvania'* Albania. I didn't need a dictionary to remind me that *Luljeta* was the name of his wife. It dawned on me that Guzim was back to his old tricks of playing on my purse strings by tugging on my heart strings, pleading penury because his wife in Albania had eaten all his money. I hardly thought the morning of Barry's wedding was the appropriate moment for my dull-witted gardener to beg for a pay rise.

"*Koita*," Guzim cried, instructing me to look and finally slowing down. "*Afto den einai arketa yia to gamo tou Barry.*" I had to agree that the offending garment certainly wasn't good enough for Barry's wedding, but was taken aback when Guzim asked if I had a shirt he could borrow. I was hardly the type of person to lend out my clothing and couldn't imagine willingly slipping my body into anything that Guzim had worn and contaminated. Borrow indeed.

"Here, tell him to take this, he can have it," Barry said, brushing past me and thrusting a perfectly decent long sleeved shirt at Guzim. The Albanian immediately prostrated himself, throwing his arms around Barry's knees and thanking him in guttural Albanian.

"It's alright mate, no need for that," Barry said, prising himself loose and escaping back into the house, clearly embarrassed by Guzim's grovelling display of gratitude.

Guzim immediately straightened up, a sly grin of triumph seeping over his features, only to be immediately replaced by ungrateful anger when he examined the donated shirt more closely.

"*Koita, einai roz,*" he spat contemptuously.

Really I couldn't believe the cheek of the man, turning up on my doorstep demanding I kit him out in a suitable shirt for the wedding, only to have Barry's generosity thrown back in my face because Guzim objected to wearing pink.

"*Nai, einai roz,*" I said, confirming it was indeed pink.

"*Tha moiazo me ton omofylofilo se roz,*" Guzim protested, saying he would look like a homosexual in pink. Seriously, I wondered if the ungrateful wretch had confused my home with a shirt shop offering a choice selection of the most fashionable colours.

"Parte to i afiste to," I snapped, my anger suddenly receding as I realised I'd correctly used the phrase 'take it or leave it,' a phrase I had painstakingly memorised but had no use for until now. My Greek certainly flowed better when I was riled.

Sensing my anger abating Guzim tried one last desperate ploy to get his hands on the contents of my wardrobe, saying *"Echete eseis esoroucha pou bora na echo?"*

My temper flared again as I understood that Guzim had just asked me if I had any underwear he could have, my outrage inspiring me to retort 'why, are you planning to strip down to your underwear at the wedding?' in what may have been perfect Greek.

"Chazi erotisi." Understanding Guzim's mumbled response of 'stupid question' I fired back in Greek 'then no one will care about your underwear.'

The sight of Guzim's hang-dog expression annoyed me so much that I screamed *"Fyge"* at the snivelling chancer, surprised that he obeyed my command to get away by scuttling off so readily. It didn't escape my notice that he kept a tight grip on the spurned pink shirt. Perhaps he was planning to sell it to one of his Albanian cronies; after all he had form. It was only after Guzim had stomped away that I recalled promising him I would have a rummage through my wardrobe for a cast-off shirt that might be suitable for the wedding.

Marigold emerged from the bedroom, rushing to hug her brother, declaring, "Oh Barry, it's your wedding day; I am so excited for you."

Before Marigold had the chance to become gushingly maudlin Barry's mobile rang. Giving her brother a warning look, Marigold told him she would never forgive him if he dashed off to give a building quote.

"It's not work, it's Cynthia," Barry said.

"Don't you dare answer it," Marigold shouted, snatching the phone from Barry's grasp. "It's bad luck to speak to the bride before the wedding."

"Don't be daft, that old wives tale is about seeing the bride, not speaking to her," Barry objected.

"Nevertheless it would be more appropriate if Victor speaks to her," Marigold insisted, thrusting the phone into my hand.

With my wife and brother-in-law both muttering "what's she saying?" over my shoulder I listened to Cynthia having hysterics, apparently on the verge of a nervous breakdown. She told me that Nikos had just telephoned her to say that his car wouldn't start and his ridiculous solution was to offer to squeeze Cynthia onto the back of his moped between him and Dina.

"I refuse to arrive for my wedding in a crash helmet, I'm having my hair done shortly and it will be ruined," Cynthia screeched. "Whoever heard of a bride with helmet hair?"

On reflection the news that Nikos' rusty old wreck wasn't up for the trip shouldn't have come as a massive surprise. Back in England his vehicle was the type one would expect to see propped up on bricks, an eyesore in an overgrown garden on a run-down estate. I had never actually seen it on the road, Nikos relying instead on his trusty old moped to zip through the village.

Attempting to calm Cynthia down I proffered a more sensible solution, saying I would ask Spiros to drive her to the *Dimarcheio*. My suggestion was met with a full blown bridezilla meltdown. To spare my eardrums I held the phone at arm's length as Cynthia yelled "Call me superstitious but I am not turning up to my wedding in a hearse."

My second suggestion that Nikos could drive her to the wedding in her car, and Barry and I would drive down to the *Dimarcheio* in Barry's van, calmed Cynthia down and met with her approval. Marigold, harder to convince that the builder's van was suitable transport for the groom to arrive in, insisted we park it well out of sight. She was still coming to terms with the lack of available limousines in the area.

With equanimity restored I decided to tackle Harold before breakfast. Making my way down the outside stone staircase I almost tripped over Cynthia's vile mutant cat. Cursing under my breath I remembered it had completely slipped my mind to ask Guzim to lock the foul feline in his shed for the day. After my earlier encounter with the crafty Albanian I refused to reduce myself to asking him for a favour.

Chapter 20

Victor Stands on his Dignity

S trolling across the village square to Harold's house I reflected that this would be the last time I thought of the property as such; by the end of the day the house would belong to Barry. Breathing deeply I inhaled the fresh scent of pine in the air, thinking it was certainly beautiful weather for the wedding, clear blue skies promising yet another idyllic Greek summer day. I was glad that we were holding the reception in the village where the temperature would be relatively cool; less sweat inducing than down on the coast.

Recalling how Cynthia's mother had tried to pressure her daughter into having a swanky reception in a coastal restaurant I was relieved that the bride had instead seen sense, realising the village was the natural choice for the celebrations. The village old-timers would be far more relaxed in the familiar taverna where there were no tourists to gawp at them. Marigold would feel far less self-conscious strutting her newly acquired Greek dance moves, along to Nikos' bouzouki, in the familiar environ.

I made a mental note to sit out the dancing, having been summarily ejected from the dance classes I had reluctantly allowed Marigold to drag me along to after standing on the odd foot too many. Looking back I considered Doreen had over reacted; she was back in open-toed sandals within the fortnight, her big toe healing nicely. Even though my wife had so insensitively accused me of lacking natural rhythm I had no wish to show her up on the dance floor. I reflected that being banned from the Greek dance class was no great loss; I'd far rather spend my time practising my Greek with Dimitris than attempt to emulate Anthony Quinn's performance in 'Zorba the Greek'. In fact if I re-called correctly the famous actor had suffered a broken foot during filming; I'd hazard a guess he broke it whilst trying to master some compli-cated step.

A couple of old men sipping tiny cups of *El-linkos kafe* and playing *tavli* outside the village shop called over to me, "*Ta leme agorata,*" see you later. I nodded with reluctant enthusiasm, wondering how they had managed to insert themselves onto the guest list. They were at most very casual acquaintances, rarely fre-quenting the taverna. It was a good job I'd re-minded Nikos not to scrimp on the canapés.

Ducking to avoid the branch of a plane tree I reached Harold's doorstep, surprised to see no sign of life. I had expected to encounter a mas-sive removal van and a coterie of removal men sweating under the weight of all Harold's be-longings. Raising the Union Jack embellished knocker on Harold's front door I reflected that I would take great delight in binning his souvenir of Old Blighty the next day and replacing it with something more tasteful and more typically Greek. I was taken aback to say the least when a dripping Harold opened the door, clad in noth-ing but too tight budgie smugglers.

"Ah, you couldn't resist the chance to have a last dip in our pool," Harold greeted me.

"It may have escaped your notice but I have never expressed the slightest interest in venturing into your pool. I have simply come to collect the keys," I said, looking down at the diminutive and rotund Brit.

"Blimey, you got out of bed on the wrong side. Give us chance to move out..."

"You are supposed to be out today," I interrupted.

"And we should be, but we can't get started moving out until the removal van turns up. Or did you expect to see my Joan lugging boxes out? She's having none of that, you know how women hate to exert themselves. Can you imagine the carry on if she broke a nail? Course you can, that wife of yours must be the same. Women, eh!"

I didn't bother to contradict him or point out that my wife wasn't so shallow to waste her thoughts on such petty things as manicures. Marigold wasn't averse to getting her hands dirty, as her flourishing pot plants testified. Although she took the precaution of slipping her hands into gardening gloves it wasn't down to vanity, but rather because she heeded my warnings about bacterial nasties such as azospirillum and clostridium maturating in the ripe breeding ground of moist soil.

"Well shouldn't you be packing?" I snapped.

"Will you hold your horses; can you see the removal van? It's not turned up yet so we're just having a last splash around while we wait. Joan's been hit hard realising she's going to have to downsize to a hot tub when we get back to England."

My heart bled for them: not. I could imagine what a tragedy it would be for the ghastly pair to have no massive swimming pool to boast about. The pair of them did love to insert the pool into their every utterance in a desperate attempt to impress any randoms; they would surely have their work cut out trying to lure their new unsuspecting neighbours into a glorified outdoor bathtub.

"Look I promised Barry I would collect the keys, what time do you expect to have them?" I asked.

"Got you running around after him, has he?" Harold snorted.

"He's rather busy today."

"Oh that's right, I forgot he's getting wed. I

tell you what Vic, our stuff should be in the van by mid-afternoon if it turns up soon, can't say quicker than that, we've a lot of worldly goods to load you know. As soon as we're sorted I'll drop the house keys off at the taverna, that's where you're having the knee-ups I heard."

Naturally I baulked in horror at such a pre-posterous proposal. The last thing we wanted was Harold and Joan gate-crashing the wedding reception and hijacking the celebration by attempting to turn it into their leaving-do.

Drawing myself up to my full height I told Harold it would be more convenient if he simply left the keys in the village shop with Tina. The odious little man visibly bristled, instantly picking up on the obvious slight; perhaps he wasn't quite as dense as I'd given him credit for.

"I'll do that Vic, wouldn't want the likes of us at your fancy do, eh. You really should get over yourself, what a tightwad throwing a party at that dump. I'm surprised that stuck-up cow Cynthia is going along with it, the way she looks down her nose at us I thought she'd have demanded a highfalutin venue. Still it's probably the best she can do at her age, settling for the first English chap that will have her who's happy to rub noses with all these Greek peasants."

Tempted though I was to punch Harold in the face, I restrained myself. I have never been the type to resort to brute violence; indeed I still harbour guilt over my reckless attack on Derek Little with the Bunsen burner. As much as I would have loved to encircle Harold's pudgy neck with my hands and squeeze with enough force for his eyes to pop out of his bulging red face, I resisted the urge.

Drawing myself to up to my full height I simply said "Keys in the shop, you horrible little oik," before turning on my heel and striding off with my dignity intact.

Chapter 21

A Testing Request

Before heading into the house, I took a deep breath to regain my composure. Although I had done a sterling job of standing on my dignity, I was nevertheless feeling rather unsettled since I do abhor confrontation, particularly with such intellectual inferiors as Harold. I wished to project a calm demeanour in front of my family and had no intention of repeating the deplorable insults that Harold had used to disparage my soon-to-be sister-in-law. If Barry caught even a whiff of what had just transpired he would likely be off like a shot to defend his bride's good name. Marigold would never forgive me if I let slip a loose lipped comment that resulted in Barry brandishing a shiner in the wedding photos.

I was pleased to walk in on a scene of cosy domestic bliss, Marigold and Barry eating breakfast together, Catastrophe nestling on Marigold's lap, Violet Burke wielding the iron over a purple frock of such vibrancy that I hoped the colour wouldn't clash with the matching mauve shirts that Barry and I would be wearing. That particular shade of purple also reminded me of the coffin lining when we'd buried Marigold's Aunty Beryl and was sure to jar with Violet Burke's sunburn.

Although I may have done a good job of masking the inner turmoil my encounter with Harold had triggered, my excessive perspiration hinted I had lost my cool. Excusing myself I made a beeline for the shower before the others could notice, responding to Barry's question if I'd collected the keys without incident with a simple thumbs-up. My body was barely wet when Marigold disturbed me by rattling the bathroom door and demanding my attention. Hastily throwing a towel around my waist I padded through to the kitchen on damp feet, presuming I was needed to allay another minor crisis as I'd done with the transport.

"Victor, what on earth were you doing in the bathroom?" Marigold asked. I considered this a superfluous question since my dripping body was answer enough. "You and Barry must leave at once. Cynthia will be here soon to collect me and Vi for our hair appointment."

"Why on earth do you need collecting, it is only a five minutes' walk to Athena's kitchen?" I said.

"Well it's just nice to do these things together, it shows support for the bride," Marigold replied. "The pair of you must clear off at once; you know that it is bad luck for you to see Cynthia before the ceremony."

"Surely that only applies to Barry," I objected.

"Well as best man you'll need to stick to Barry like a limpet and make sure he turns up on time," Marigold argued.

"I can stick to him here," I said.

"Why must you turn this into an argument, I have just told you that Cynthia is on her way over. You have to make yourselves scarce anyway as us girls will all be getting ready here together once we've had our hair done."

"But Cynthia doesn't even live here, why can't she throw her dress on over at Milton's house?"

Firing a withering look in my direction Marigold said, "Oh Victor, must you be so obtuse, surely you know that it is tradition for the bride to get ready with her bridesmaids."

"But Cynthia isn't having any bridesmaids...or has she roped you and mother in at the last moment?"

"Must you take everything so literally, it was just a figure of speech?"

"It's okay Sis, we'll get out of your hair. It will be nice for Cynthia to have your company while you all get ready together, especially if she has wedding nerves. Me and Victor can pop over to Vangelis' house and get suited up there," Barry said.

"Barry, sometimes you can be as dense as Victor," Marigold fired at her brother. "You can't possibly get ready at Vangelis' house as we're having our hair done in the kitchen there."

"Okay, we'll go to Spiros' place instead, I'm sure he won't mind letting us getting ready there, whatever makes you happy Sis." I was pleased that Barry didn't allow Marigold's abrupt tone to get under his skin, though rather taken aback when he added with a voice laden with criticism, "How come you didn't have all this on your list Victor, I thought you were organising all the fine details?"

"Well I told him a hundred times that Cynthia was getting ready here," Marigold said unconvincingly. I knew for a fact this was the first that I'd ever heard of it.

"Come on Victor, grab your suit and we'll head over to Spiros' place," Barry urged.

"It may have escaped your notice but I'm rather underdressed. I have no intention of making myself a laughing stock by traipsing through the village clad in nothing but a towel."

"Barry, you go now in case Cynthia arrives, Victor will catch you up when he's more suitable attired," Marigold ordered, throwing his wedding suit at him and practically pushing Barry out of the house.

Having successfully dispatched her brother Marigold suddenly changed her tune, instructing me to hang around whilst she went down to the garden to raid her flowering pot plants for suitable groom and best man boutonnieres.

"I'll come with you," Violet Burke announced.

"I'm not sure about those plastic cherries on my hat; perhaps a fresh flower would give it a more weddingly look."

I was relieved to be rid of them since I planned to return to my shower and dress in my wedding suit, before strolling over to join Barry. There was clearly no need for Barry and me to buy into the girly nonsense of getting ready together. My immediate plan to jump into the shower was thwarted by Cynthia's arrival. Cradling her vile mutant cat which I had failed to dispose of in Guzim's shed, Cynthia launched into a self-obsessed monologue with no regard at all to the fact that I was standing there in nothing but a towel. I listened with half an ear as she prattled on mindlessly, hoping that Barry would like her dress and worrying there would be enough canapés to go round.

Cynthia abruptly dropped the cat mid-sentence and made a dash for the bathroom. Apparently she was so desperate that she didn't have time to adhere to the niceties of closing the door, thus subjecting me to the grotesque sounds of her breakfast being hurled up. At least she had the grace to grovel an apology when she returned ashen-faced, her wan complexion prompting me to solicitously ask if I should summon a doctor or if she had simply been overcome by a sickly bout of bridal nerves.

"I've a feeling it may be more than nerves Victor," Cynthia said, her paleness replaced with a blush. "I've been feeling off colour and queasy all week. It's probably nothing but...Victor, could I ask you the most enormous favour?"

"Of course," I replied, knowing Barry would expect no less of me.

"Could you pop into the pharmacy and buy a pregnancy testing kit? Discreetly of course, perhaps best wait until the place is empty, and don't say anything to Barry or Marigold."

I must confess to being rather gob-smacked by Cynthia's request, blurting out something along the lines of 'I'd really rather not.' I didn't relish the idea of sneaking around behind Barry and Marigold's backs, and I had my reputation to consider. I could just imagine the ridiculous conclusions people would jump to if word got out that I had been seen purchasing such an incendiary item. Word would spread like wildfire through the village; any gullible fools who had listened to Despina's gossipmongering about me carrying on with Cynthia might assume there was truth to the rumours. After all it is patently obvious that Marigold is well past requiring such a test, even though she does look quite marvellous for her age.

"I know that it's asking a lot Victor, but I'd really appreciate it and there is no one else I could trust to be discreet," Cynthia pleaded before making another mad dash to the bathroom, once again assailing my ears with the sounds of copious vomiting.

As I busied myself grating some fresh ginger and adding it to cup of hot water with half a lemon to counteract Cynthia's nausea, I recalled Marigold telling me that weddings could be very stressful. It struck me that Cynthia was likely just having a bridezilla breakdown and it may well calm her nerves if I humoured her. Surely the woman couldn't seriously imagine she had a bun in the oven, after all she must be the wrong side of forty and was most likely delusional.

Returning from the bathroom Cynthia wordlessly accepted the mug of ginger and lemon, sighing in relief when I promised to call in the pharmacy on my way to meet Barry. Whether it was my promise or the ginger concoction, the colour had begun to return to Cynthia's cheeks by the time Marigold and my mother returned bearing sunflowers.

"Are you excited?" Marigold gushed, throwing her arms around Cynthia.

"I was a bag of nerves when I got here but Victor has done a wonderful job of calming me down," Cynthia said, thanking me with her eyes.

"I'm not sure about this sunflower for my hat, orange might clash. Happen I'll stick with the plastic cherries," Violet Burke said before staring at Cynthia and adding, "You look a bit washed out girl."

"I'm fine, just wedding jitters. Milton is a bit off colour though, he and Edna won't be able to make it to the wedding, such a disappointment," Cynthia revealed.

"Has he summoned a doctor?" I enquired.

"Really Victor, are you being deliberately obtuse?" Marigold hissed. "There's nothing the matter with Milton, he's clearly swerving the wedding to avoid your mother and to make sure he doesn't make a fool of himself in front of Edna."

"Oh well, that just means more canapés for the rest of us," Violet Burke said pragmatically.

Chapter 22

A Last Minute Dash to the Wedding

A fter skulking suspiciously outside the pharmacy until the last of the elderly customers had filled their prescriptions, I finally struck up the courage to enter. Done up in my best bib and tucker for the wedding I already felt conspicuous, an uncomfortable state that was heightened by the nature of my delicate mission. It was not a shop I was in the habit of frequenting; in fact I went out of my way to avoid it since I consider such places are potential petri dishes for communicable germs.

Apart from the inevitable hypochondriac with imaginary symptoms, the majority of the clientele are likely symptomatic with something nasty identified by a medic.

I could count on one hand the number of times I had been in: a couple of times for bottles of Gaviscon for heartburn relief, once for an anti-fungal cream to counter the dermatophytosis I had contracted from sticking my hands in the contaminated mittens Guzim's wife Luljeta spun from loose rabbit hairs, and the previous day to purchase strong painkillers for Marigold's toothache since the village store *Depon* proved useless, my wife being in dire need of something stronger than paracetamol.

I was on no more than polite nodding terms with the pharmacist on duty, a rather chic woman in her mid-forties. I knew from Spiros that she lived in a rather grand villa on the coast, boasting electric gates and a lavish swimming pool. Apparently her husband was worth a small fortune, but she refused to rest idly on his riches, preferring to work three days a week in the family business her father had established.

Reluctant to voice my reason for dropping in, I loitered, trying not to stand out like a sore thumb, pretending to take an interest in the goods on the shelves. In truth I was as embarrassed as a schoolboy plucking up the nerve to buy his first packet of condoms. I would have much preferred the pharmacist's father to be on duty rather than make such a personal and intimate purchase from a woman. Deciding that the product I needed would be less conspicuous if I included it amongst a few other items, I randomly selected a strawberry exfoliating face mask and a packet of cough sweets before approaching the counter. After pulling out my handy English to Greek pocket dictionary and consulting the pages I said *"Tha ithela ena kit dokimis enkymosynis,"* with as much nonchalance as I could muster. I could feel my face flushing; after all this was one Greek sentence I had never envisaged uttering.

The pharmacist raised a questioning eyebrow before saying in English "You want the pregnancy test?" just as the door opened and Panos marched in. I flushed even redder in utter mortification until it dawned on me that his lack of English meant that Panos was clueless to the meaning of the words she had voiced.

"Yes please," I replied, crossing my fingers that she would simply slip the requested item discreetly into a bag.

"I recommend this one for the accuracy," the pharmacist said, holding a slim blue box aloft before grabbing a pink box and adding "But this one costs less."

"Yes, whatever you recommend, sorry I'm in a hurry," I replied in English, in too much of a rush to escape before Panos cornered me or spotted the test to bother attempting to converse in Greek. Too late; I felt Panos' hand bearing down on my shoulder.

"*Ti kaneis edo Victor?*" the welly wearing farmer greeted me, asking what I was doing there.

"*Agorazo afto…*" I replied, waving the face mask in his face and telling him I was buying it.

"*Ah, yia ton yos sou.*" I had no idea why Panos presumed the fruity face mask was for my son, but I nodded in agreement, desperate to get away in case the pharmacist indiscreetly announced my more delicate purchase. Taking a deep breath as she rang up my goods I reasoned that pharmacists were surely duty bound by the same patient confidentiality as other medical professionals.

"*Eimai edo yia na agoraso kati yia ton kondyloto mou,*" Panos boomed. I understood that he was telling me he was here to buy something, but the something proved elusive since I had no clue what a *kondyloto* was.

Spotting my puzzled expression the pharmacist kindly filled me in, telling me that Panos needed something for his wart. As I handed over my money I reflected that she hadn't technically broken patient confidentiality since Panos was the first one to bring up his personally embarrassing complaint. The farmer's condition reinforced my natural reluctance to frequent the pharmacy due to the risk of contracting a communicable condition, though to be fair he could have picked it up from the wart faced old harridan Despina who until recently had been serving in the village shop. Making a mental note to warn the family to avoid getting close to Panos during the celebrations in case his wart was of the contagious variety, I hastily added a bottle of anti-bacterial hand sanitiser to my purchases.

"Se des sto gamo," Panos called after me as I fled, saying he would see me at the wedding.

I was still feeling decidedly flustered when I arrived at Spiros' house. I inwardly cursed Cynthia for putting me in such an embarrassing predicament, way beyond my comfort zone. I hoped that she planned to reimburse me for the outrageously expensive pregnancy test. Although her plea that I not mention anything to Barry didn't sit well with me, nevertheless I felt duty bound to honour my promise to keep schtum.

Spiros greeted me by announcing "the Barry is in the bathroom."

"Showering and dressing," I guessed hopefully since time was getting on.

"He interrogate the washing machine, there is the bad smell behind it."

"He needs to be getting ready, it's nearly time for the off," I said impatiently, dismissing Spiros' absurd use of the word interrogate; this wasn't the time to delve into his use of the English language.

"But Victor you took the time to go the shopping, I see you come from the pharmacy," Spiros countered.

Realising I was clutching the brown paper bag containing the unmentionable item Cynthia had requested, I reached in to grab the strawberry exfoliating face mask before discreetly slipping the bag into my inside suit pocket. Handing the small sachet of face gunk to Spiros I improvised, saying "I stopped in to buy this small thank you gift for accommodating us at the last moment."

Peering at the face mask curiously Spiros replied "This is the very thoughtful of you Victor, I will to look forward to trying this new English food."

"It's not..." I began before stopping mid-sentence. Consuming the face mask was unlikely to give Spiros an upset stomach; after all it was packed with strawberry goodness.

"Victor, I must to bring the uncle to the wedding, I think the Kyria Kompogiannopoulou to sit with him at the house but she is go to the wedding too."

"It will probably do Leo good to get out," I said, wondering how Kyria Kompogiannopoulou had managed to wangle an invitation to the wedding: we barely knew the woman, though she had been very accommodating in allowing Marigold access to her toilet when we'd been menaced by a sheep outside her house.

Holding something decidedly pungent at arm's length, Barry joined us on the doorstep, telling Spiros "this was the source of the bad smell; you need to put some poison down mate." On closer inspection I realised that Barry was swinging a dead mouse by its tail. Still at least he had changed into his suit and would look suitably groom like as soon as he disposed of the festering rodent.

"I have your boutonniere," I said, shoving the sunflower into Barry's lapel. Although it was a tad over-sized it provided a fitting final touch; being more rustic than debonair it definitely suited Barry's personality.

Consulting his watch Barry said "according to your timetable we should be setting off any minute now."

"Indeed. Have you double checked that you have everything Barry?"

"The only thing I need is my bride," Barry quipped. "What about you Victor, do you have the ring?"

"Of course, I'm hardly likely to forget such an important detail," I assured him, double checking my pockets anyway and finding nothing there but the inevitable dictionary, the ring box, a bag of cough sweets, a bottle of hand sanitiser, and the pregnancy testing kit.

"I don't believe it, I must have left my best man's speech at the house...be back in two ticks Barry," I promised, practically breaking into an unseemly jog in my rush to retrieve the papers.

With the hastily grabbed speech in hand I

bolted back outside, panting heavily, bumping slap-bang into Cynthia, Marigold and my mother returning from having their hair done.

"Victor, what on earth are you doing hanging around here, surely you and Barry ought to be making your way to the *Dimarcheio* by now?" Marigold chided.

"I came back for my speech, worry not my darling, we're just off now," I assured her, remembering to take the time to tell the trio that their hair looked perfectly delightful. In truth Cynthia's hair looked more than a tad stiff; I surmised that Athena had gone way overboard with the hairspray. I dreaded to think what combination of vile toxins must have leaked out from the aerosol lacquer to contaminate the contents of her kitchen. Still at least Cynthia's rigid hair would stay in place if the transport arrangements should go wrong at the last moment and she was reduced to riding pillion on Nikos' moped.

Seemingly forgetting that I was meant to be hurrying off, Marigold thrust a high-heeled shoe under my nose. "Look at this, Athena wrote the name of every unmarried woman on the sole of Cynthia's wedding shoe. It's a Greek tradition. It is supposed to be the names of the bridesmaids, but as there aren't any Athena wrote Sampaguita, Litsa, Violet, Kyria Maria and Kyria Komp…er…oogilou."

"Why?" I asked, genuinely curious about this quaint Greek custom, but in too much of a rush to correct Marigold's dire pronunciation of Kyria Kompogiannopoulou.

"Well whoever's name is the first to be rubbed off will be the next to be married," Marigold explained.

"I thought it was whichever name was still left at the end of the day would snag a husband," Cynthia argued.

"Well it's one or the other," Marigold said impatiently.

"I hope it's the name of that nice little Filipino girl that gets rubbed off because I've no plans to saddle myself with another husband," my mother snorted.

"Victor, you need to stop dawdling," Marigold reminded me, overlooking the fact that she was the one who had detained me with the shoe saga. Cynthia tried to catch my eye but I skilfully avoided it, knowing I could not pass the little blue box to her without rousing Marigold's curiosity.

"I'm going, see you at the *Dimarcheio*," I

said, hastening back to Barry who was by now waiting around the corner in his van, impatiently revving the engine.

My heart sank at the sight of the builder's van; its grimy exterior was well overdue a rigorous cleaning. I reflected that Barry's time would have been better spent taking a hosepipe to his vehicle rather than rummaging around behind Spiros' washing machine in search of rotting rodents. Cringing at the sight of a layer of sawdust coating the seat I dragged Barry out of the van, using a dustpan and brush he kept in the footwell to give his suit a thorough dusting down. Marigold would have kittens if I allowed Barry to turn up for his wedding covered in shavings and wood chippings.

Seated on black plastic bin bags to preserve our pristine appearance we made our way to the *Dimarcheio*, Barry grumbling that if he'd known I was going to make such a fuss over a bit of dirt he would have accepted Spiros' offer to take us in the back of the immaculately clean hearse.

Chapter 23

Snaring the Mayor

After ditching the dirty van in a side street, we made our way to the *Dimarcheio* with plenty of time to spare. The building was bustling with everyday folk going about their business in various offices, but we headed directly into the room that had been allocated for the service. The boys had done an excellent job of strategically placing the plastic floral blooms, giving the ornate room a definite wedding air; I reflected that artificial flowers had their advantages as they wouldn't be magnets for flying insects. Of course, our freshly cut sunflowers still posed a possible hazard; the service could likely turn into a farce if the odd wasp or two dive-bombed our boutonnieres.

A youngish man in a less than pristine suit and tie was arranging some papers on the dais facing the circular rows of raised seating. I was rather taken aback by the relative youth of the mayor, having expected him to be of more mature years; nevertheless I approached him, eager to finally make his acquaintance. I wasn't above ingratiating myself if it resulted in my being appointed to lead a local taskforce to tackle the disgusting state of the public bins.

"Ha, you are the mistake, I am not the mayor," the young man corrected me, his wide smile indicating my assumption had pleased him; no doubt he had lofty ambitions in that direction. "He will to been here shortly for the wedding service. He speak little the English so any the question please put to the me."

"We'd appreciate it if you could just talk us through what to expect, it is the first time that either of us has attended a Greek wedding," I said.

"I thought you went to the wedding of Kostis and Eleni," Barry piped up.

"Yes, but that was a church-do, not a civil service," I pointed out.

"The church marriage go on much the time, much the too long. Here the service is the very nice and the short, just the five minute and done. After doing the service the couple go with the, how you say in the English, the witless, up the stair to make the legal document," the young man explained.

"I think you mean the witnesses," Barry corrected, clearly on the ball.

"*Nai, dyo martyres*," the young man confirmed in Greek, Barry hissing in my ear "it sounds like a couple of martyrs off to the slaughter."

"You have the translator?" the young man asked.

"No, we thought we'd go for the full Greek experience," Barry replied, adding "my bride's quite good with the Greek lingo."

Stifling a laugh I reflected that this was one occasion when Barry's builder's Greek would prove useless.

"Ah, here is the mayor now, you want me to intro you?"

"That would be splendid," I said, rather taken aback to note the distinctly shabby appearance of the esteemed local dignitary, the mayor being a tall fat man with an obvious comb-over. The shirt straining over his gut sported a visibly frayed collar and was tucked into a pair of blue jeans that had seen better days. I pondered if there was a possibly polite way of suggesting the young man lend the mayor his tie since the mayor appeared to favour the more casual look.

Shaking our hands the mayor said *"poios einai o gampros?"* asking which one of us was the groom.

"Mou," Barry confirmed.

"Kai esi?" the mayor asked, wanting to know who I was.

"Eimai o koubaros," I replied, using the Greek word for best man.

The mayor reeled off some spiel at a speed too quickly for me to comprehend. Fortunately the young man was eminently capable of keeping up a running translation whilst the mayor continued to speak without pausing for breath.

"He is the honour to marry the two tourists..."

"Technically they aren't tourists as they both live here, they are European citizens with Greek residency," I interrupted.

"And he want to make the clear there to be absolutely the no throwing, how to say in the English, the *komfeti*."

"Confetti," Barry obligingly translated.

"And no the throwing the rice, it will to encourage the cat ferals to congregate on the steps outside," the young man continued.

"Got it, no rice and no confetti," Barry responded. "That will please Marigold; she thinks that chucking stuff at the bride is terribly vulgar."

"Please convey to the mayor that I wholeheartedly applaud his no rice policy, it is a disgustingly insanitary practice," I added.

"Good yes," the mayor said with a broad smile, his selective use of English reminding me of Vasos. I suppressed an involuntary giggle, imagining the mayor throwing the words 'beautiful towel' in for good measure.

"Could you tell the mayor that we would be most honoured if he'd like to join us at the wedding festivities in Meli after the service," I requested, thinking it would be an excellent opportunity to corner him about my meticulous plans relating to bin hygiene and my innovative sanitising suggestions.

The young man conferred with the mayor

before saying, "He ask if you to grill the meat."

"Of course, Nikos is spit roasting a lamb, and there will also be a wonderful selection of canapés," I confirmed.

"He will to try to attend if he can make free the time."

"Excellent," I said, delighted to have snared such an esteemed dignitary for the occasion. I hoped his schedule allowed for him to arrive before all the canapés had been snagged, but if necessary, I was prepared to snatch any choice ones out of the hands of any uninvited freeloaders.

Chapter 24

Here Comes the Bride

Shuffling nervously Barry muttered impatiently, "What's the time Victor?"

"Get a grip Barry; it's barely twenty seconds since the last time you asked."

"This getting here early isn't good for my nerves, I'm on the verge of breaking out in a cold sweat," Barry complained.

"Just take deep breaths," I advised.

The two of us were standing rather stiffly in front of the dais as though it was a substitute altar. The room was deserted, the mayor having slunk outside for a cigarette.

"Relax, look the guests are beginning to arrive," I said as Spiros, Sampaguita and Spiros' Uncle Leo filed in. Leo took in his surroundings with interest, indicating he may be enjoying one of his lucid phases. I was pleased to see they were all suitably turned out in their Sunday best for the occasion. After making sure that Sampaguita and Leo were seated comfortably, Spiros headed over. Rolling his eyes, he hissed "Your the mother try to get in the hearse, I think she to confuse it with the limousine."

"Any sign of Marigold?"

"The Benjamin parking the Punto. Excuse me, I must to greet the Papas Andreas, you are much the honour he turn up here Barry, this is not the church."

Swivelling around, I noticed Papas Andreas accompanying our neighbour, his mother Kyria Maria. The pair of them hadn't bothered to make the slightest effort, dressed in their usual gloomy garb despite the celebratory nature of the occasion, she in her customary black widow's weeds, the Papas in his everyday ankle-length black cassock, the legs of his jeans poking out conspicuously beneath the hemline.

"The Papas looks a bit different," Barry observed. "He's done something to his beard; it's not as unruly as usual."

"Perhaps he invested in an electric beard trimmer," I suggested, recalling how Marigold had been keen to gift him one for performing our house blessing ceremony. My wife would be pleased that the local clergyman was experimenting with personal grooming. She could never quite comprehend why he didn't simply break with tradition and go with the clean shaven look, convinced it would take years off him.

"Litsa has made it, she's out of the hospital," I nudged Barry, pleased to see the elderly lady hobbling in with the aid of her stick. Unlike Kyria Maria she had dressed up for the occasion, her usual black widow's weeds replaced with a shapeless brown dress patterned with yellow daisies, and a matching headscarf. Still bearing the brunt of her bruises, I could see the pain etched on her tired face. Her features transformed into a creased yet radiant smile when Barry blew her a kiss and Spiros rushed over to assist her to a seat. Litsa budged up to accommodate Kyria Kompogiannopoulou who for some inexplicable reason came armed with her knitting. I considered she had perhaps confused the civil service with a church one, expecting it to drag on for hours. As soon as she sat down she was overcome with a nasty bout of coughing which showed no sign of abating.

Catching Spiros' eye I beckoned him over, directing him to give the packet of cough sweets I had purchased earlier to Kyria Kompogiannopoulou. The crinkling of sweet wrappers would be less intrusive than the sound of hacking coughing during the service. I hoped the woman didn't have anything contagious; it really would be too much if she passed some ghastly germs to our guests, particularly since I still had no clue how she had managed to wangle herself an invitation.

I watched with interest as more guests began to file in. I hardly recognised Dina; shimmering in a very smart skirt suit in vibrant orange and dripping in gold jewellery, she presented a completely different image to her usual one of kitchen skivvy. Dina came over to smother me in a motherly embrace, whispering that Eleni hadn't wanted to risk the journey in case the potholes sent her into labour, and reassuring Barry that Nikos and Cynthia were on their way.

Vangelis and Athena arrived together, the local builder and his wife so done up in their fancy threads that I hardly recognised them. I reflected that Athena must bulk buy cans of hairspray by the pallet load. Even after liberally spraying Cynthia, her own elaborate coiffure was so stiffly styled it looked as though she'd gone mad with the starch. Panos arrived, having changed out of his farming clobber into a dated suit; ditching the ubiquitous wellies and pairing the suit with trainers.

"Spread the word to avoid close contact with Panos," I hissed at Barry. He raised a questioning eyebrow. "Warts," I clarified.

Guzim slunk in, managing to look shabby and shifty despite modelling Barry's smart pink shirt. Pairing the shirt with baggy grey jogging trousers was hardly a fashion success, and I wondered if his decision to wear black socks with flip flops was his way of having a personal dig at me since we had parted on rather bad terms that morning. Having presumed Guzim would skip the service due to work commitments and only turn up at the reception to fill up on free food, I reflected that his presence was quite the noble gesture, considering how much he needed the cash to send to Albania. Perhaps

I would have a rummage through my wardrobe for suitable cast-offs; such an altruistic gesture on my part would demonstrate that there were no hard feelings.

Doreen and Norman arrived looking decidedly ordinary next to the flashy Greeks. Slipping into the seats next to Athena they appeared decidedly out of their element, Doreen completely overshadowed by Athena's flamboyant finery. I reflected that their obvious discomfort was likely down to unfamiliarity with the situation; not being able to understand a word of Greek they were probably clueless what to expect. At least our earlier chat with the mayor had given us a bit of a heads-up.

"Phew, I feel better now that Marigold's here," Barry said as my wife walked in with the boys. I felt a surge of pride in my family. Marigold looked the picture of elegance in a fitted emerald green dress, Benjamin and his partner smartly kitted out in lightweight summer suits, sunflowers adorning their lapels. Rushing over to embrace her brother and make a last minute adjustment to his tie, Marigold gushed "You look so handsome Barry."

Clearing my throat in the hope of receiving a similar compliment merely provoked my wife into saying "I do hope you haven't caught that nasty cough from Kyria Kompo...do...lou..,"

"Kompogiannopoulou," I reminded her, having swotted up on the correct pronunciation of the tongue-twister name.

"Athena just wrote the first part on Cynthia's shoe, there wouldn't have been any room left for the names of the other single women if she'd scrawled the whole thing. Oh good grief, have you seen your mother's hat, if she sits in the front row she will block everyone's view of the ceremony," Marigold said, dashing off to steer my mother away from a front row seat.

Violet Burke cut a commanding figure, the purple frock clinging snugly to her bulbous frame, a matching lace bolero adding an almost glamorous finishing touch. It was impossible to tell if Athena had sprayed her hair immovably since it was obscured by the enormous lime green monstrosity perched on her head, embellished with plastic cherries dangling over her forehead.

The room was abuzz with noisy chatter, the Greeks casting judgement on other people's outfits and speculating on the size of Cynthia's *proika*, even though my research revealed that the centuries-old tradition of a marriage dowry had been illegal for the last two decades. Surveying the guests I was surprised to notice Tiffany sitting amongst them, though it took me a minute to recognise her in civvies rather than orange polyester. Guessing that Cynthia must have invited her in a moment of weakness I wondered if she knew that the reception was being held in our local taverna, the same taverna I had deliberately misrepresented as a cockroach infested dump riddled with E-coli and hostile locals. Her unexpected presence became more explanatory when I noticed Sakis sitting off to one side; Tiffany could be a tad stalkish when it came to the handsome moustached coach driver.

Still tieless, the mayor wandered back in reeking of cigarette smoke. He joined us briefly at the dais before spotting Papas Andreas amongst the guests and rushing over to kiss him. I hoped that our guest list suitably impressed the mayor; it may make him less inclined to consider us tourists. Spiros, hovering in the doorway as though pondering if he had enough time to nip out for a cigarette, attracted everyone's attention by loudly declaring *"i nyfi."* With the announcement that the bride was here the mayor took his position in front of the dais and Barry stopped shaking, squaring his shoulders and swivelling round to watch his beloved's entrance.

Making her entrance on Nikos' arm Cynthia presented the image of a shyly radiant bride. Even though she hadn't opted for a traditional poufy wedding gown, the off-the-peg summer dress she was wearing looked suitably bridal, stylishly simple in off-white lace. Although certainly not an expert on women's clothing I do believe the fashion experts would describe the style as an A-line midi. Carrying a delicate bouquet of garden blue daisies Cynthia walked very slowly towards Barry, most likely watching her step because her view of the groom was obscured by the borrowed bridal veil. Nikos, resplendent in a smart black suit and maroon tie, walked with the confidence of a movie star. It was the first time I had seen him completely clean shaven and the lack of stubble accentuated his handsome features and twinkling eyes.

Barry beamed from ear to ear as his bride joined him and Nikos lifted the stunning veil to her reveal her smiling face. With Cynthia's features suffused in joy it struck me that perhaps I had been a tad hasty presuming she was past her child bearing years.

Chapter 25

One for the Album

After all the anticipation of the ceremony the whole thing was over in a matter of minutes, the mayor having sped through the formalities as though desperate to slink off outside for another cigarette. If that was his intention it was thwarted when Cynthia told him in hesitant Greek that they would like to read the personal vows they had written for the occasion. The mayor was forced to stand around like a spare part whilst Cynthia and Barry dragged the proceedings out by making heartfelt promises to one another in a language the dignitary could not understand. The moment the happy couple shared an intimate kiss the room erupted in rowdy applause and the mayor legged it, lighting up even before he'd escaped the building.

"Come, I show you where to make the legal," Spiros offered, leading the way upstairs, Marigold and I in our official capacity as witnesses following the bride and groom. A disorderly line of people obstructed the open office doorway, a couple of council employees attending to mundane business. Taking charge, Spiros pushed through, announcing he had a pair of newlyweds needing to sign their formal paperwork. The waiting people turned eagerly to stare at the bride and groom, offering their congratulations and generously insisting they push in to the front of the queue. As Barry and Cynthia signed the necessary paperwork, Spiros beckoned for me and Marigold to join them, saying "*diavatiria.*"

I exchanged a worried glance with Marigold. Having neglected to bring my passport I expected my wife to kick off since we needed to prove our identity as witnesses; however I was spared a lecture since Marigold had also forgotten to bring along this vital document.

"It's not like you to be so disorganised Victor," Barry observed.

"I always carry it when I'm driving…course today you were at the wheel," I offered as a rather lame excuse.

"Victor, go the down to see if any the other have the *diavatiria*, they can to witness instead the you," Spiros instructed.

"Righto, I'll go and try and round up two witnesses with passports," I agreed, hoping against hope that two of the guests were carrying the necessary identification. It would hardly be a good start to the festivities if the bride and groom were forced to hang around at the *Dimarcheio* whilst I nipped back to Meli for our passports.

The guests were beginning to file out of the room where the service had taken place and congregate on the steps outside where Adam planned to gather everyone for the photographs; his artful expertise with the camera had saved a small fortune on hiring a professional. Rushing over to Benjamin I explained my dilemma, relieved when he instantly came to the rescue by saying he would stand in as a witness. Luckily he had his passport tucked into his inside pocket because he'd taken the wheel of the Punto. Alas Adam had come out without his, but Violet Burke was able to step in as the second witness when she discovered her passport during a quick rummage through her handbag.

The Greeks that had obligingly allowed us to push in gawped at the ginormous lime green thing perched on Violet Burke's head, as though it was the first time they had ever encountered a hat. Clearly mistaking their transfixed gazes for envy, my mother adjusted the monstrosity to a jaunty angle, nearly taking Cynthia's eye out with a plastic cherry when she bent over to scrawl her signature on the paperwork.

Once the formalities were out of the way Cynthia gushed excitedly, "We're legally married. Oh Barry, I'm so happy."

"I couldn't make head nor tail of the service, did we do the 'till death do us part' bit?" Barry asked.

Being none the wiser than my brother-in-law as to the finer details of what had actually gone down, I jokingly added, "And did Cynthia promise to obey you?"

"I don't mind if I did, after all Barry is my husband now," Cynthia said proudly. "I can't tell you what a relief it is to have finally ditched the Trout moniker."

"I thought your name was Troot," Violet Burke blurted.

The Greeks burst into another spontaneous round of applause when Barry and Cynthia appeared on the steps outside the *Dimarcheio*. From the corner of my eye I spotted Tiffany preparing to shower the newlyweds with a handful of rice.

"That's not allowed, the mayor has banned it," I shouted, hurling myself on Tiffany before she had chance to perfect her throw. I could hardly expect the mayor to take my proposals for sanitary improvements seriously if I allowed the steps of the town hall to be littered in defiance of his instructions.

"But throwing rice is like lucky, I read that it symbolises like fertility," Tiffany protested.

"It is an insanitary practice that encourages vermin," I countered crossly, Tiffany's words reminding me that Cynthia's pregnancy testing kit was burning a hole in my inside pocket.

"Oh, I never like thought of that, I still have like nightmares about cockroaches," Tiffany shuddered.

"It's certainly an excellent turn out," Marigold said as I joined her in the middle of the bustling group with Adam attempting to direct the guests for the photographs; being unable to speak a word of Greek he certainly had his work cut out. "It's nice to see how popular Barry is with the locals considering how new to the area he is."

"Very encouraging. And I think I managed to persuade the mayor to join us at the reception," I boasted.

"What a terrible scruff, you think he'd have made more of an effort," Marigold scoffed.

"Scruffy he may be but he is undoubtedly a man of importance. Why is Cynthia limping," I asked.

"It's probably down to the coin that Dina stuffed into her shoe. Dina said it was a tradition symbolising prosperity, but it must be terribly awkward for Cynthia to move comfortably with a two euro coin wedged under her toes."

Our conversation was interrupted by Adam manoeuvring us into position for a photograph with the bride and groom. "Just the immediate family in this one," Adam directed, holding his hands up in frustration when hordes of Greeks tried to push their way into the shot.

"*Mono tin oikoyeneia,*" I called out helpfully.

The Greeks stepped out of the way, replaced by Violet Burke bowling her way to the front: the photograph of Cynthia with her head obscured by my mother's hat never made it into the album.

I duly translated when Adam called for a group shot and everyone scrunched together, Panos obligingly offering to take charge of the camera so that Adam could be included in the picture: the photographs of Barry missing his head, and Panos' bungled shot of his own trainers, were another couple that didn't make it into the album.

Kyria Maria introduced us to the novel and disgusting tradition of *ftou ftou*; old women spitting at the bride for good luck. Our vexatious neighbour couldn't persuade Dina, Litsa or Kyria Kompogiannopoulou to join her in firing off their spittle, and fortunately for Cynthia, Maria's aim was off. However Adam was poised with camera ready to capture the moment when Kyria Maria's spit missed Cynthia and landed on Tiffany. The superb shot is so artfully executed that Barry framed the portrait; to this day it takes pride of place in his downstairs lavatory. The copy we have made it into the album.

As everyone posed and preened for the photographs Tiffany sidled up to Adam with a predatory look, placing a proprietary hand on his arm and loudly suggesting "You should like take pictures of everyone on the beach like the tourists do, it would be a like romantic setting." Unsure how to respond, Adam looked to me for guidance.

"We don't want to look like tourists, we live here," I explained to Tiffany, extracting her possessive hand from my practically son-in-law's arm and discreetly hissing, "Keep your claws off Adam, he's my son's boyfriend."

"Well said darling, the last thing I want is to get sand in my tights or risk this bunch of pensioners coming down with sunstroke," Marigold said approvingly. "I think we should be making a move up to the taverna now, will you round everyone up?"

When I announced it was time to make our way to the taverna in Meli and continue the festivities there, everyone made a dash for their vehicles. I held back to make sure that all our guests had some form of transportation and to ensure we didn't leave any stragglers behind. As I started to leave I noticed with dismay that the steps were littered with *koufeta*, the traditional sugared almonds that feature in many Greek celebrations. It appeared that despite my watchful eye someone had managed to throw the sugary treats at the newlyweds. Sighing with frustration I began to scoop them up; it wouldn't do my reputation any good if any of the local ferals choked on a random *koufeta*.

Chapter 26

Canapé Confusion

S quashed uncomfortably between Marigold and my mother in the back seat of the Punto I felt grateful that Milton had warned me about the noisy Greek custom of wedding guests driving in convoy from the service to the reception, with horns blasting. Forewarned, I had taken the precaution of putting a set of earplugs into the glove box. Unfortunately Violet Burke claimed her need for peace and quiet was greater than mine, requisitioning said earplugs before I had chance to bung them in my ears. The cacophonous din proved as ear-splitting as I had feared, though Barry appeared to appreciate it; then again my brother-in-law has always been tone deaf.

Although it is not customary for the groom to drive himself and his bride to the wedding reception, I refused to risk taking the wheel since I had no identification on me to flash at the police if we were pulled over. I had no wish to flout the law; even though my budding relationship with the mayor looked promising, I felt it was a tad too soon in our acquaintance to ask him to intercede with the local constabulary should I suffer the indignity of being arrested.

Cynthia's refusal to sit on a plastic bin bag in Barry's van made a mockery of her so recently avowed intent to obey her husband, but I reluctantly agreed it wouldn't do if she got sawdust or wood chippings on the borrowed veil; after all it was a precious heirloom. Thus the five of us ended up in the Punto with Barry at the wheel, whilst Benjamin and Adam made their way back to Meli in the filthy builder's van.

Reaching the first hill the convoy of cars drew to an agonisingly slow crawl. I reflected that if the driver of the first vehicle stuck behind whatever was obstructing our progress blasted his horn it would make not the slightest difference, since every horn in the convoy was being actively blasted.

"What's the hold up?" Violet Burke demanded, sticking her head out of the window.

"Careful mother, you don't want to lose your hat," I advised.

"What, what are you saying Victor?" my mother shouted, unable to hear anything with the ear plugs bunged firmly in place.

Craning her neck out of the other window Marigold announced "It looks as though the convoy can't overtake a slow moving moped, the road is too narrow and of course there are so many hair-pin bends."

Contorting my body I leaned across Marigold. Sticking my head out of the window I instantly recognised Guzim's tatty moped creeping up the hill, belching exhaust fumes over the rest of the convoy. It appeared the Albanian had got a head start on the other vehicles, creating the traffic jam. When the convoy came to a grinding halt I clambered out of the Punto to see what was happening: to my amusement I witnessed Vangelis chucking Guzim's moped into the back of his pick-up in a presumably desperate attempt to clear the blockage from the road.

Although Vangelis must have been sorely tempted to leave the Albanian behind, he gave him a leg-up into the back of the pick-up.

The din of the horns was replaced by animated chatter when we finally reached Meli. The interior of the taverna looked oddly bereft, having been stripped of every table and chair. They had been pushed together with all the outdoor furniture to form two long rows of tables outside, the available seating far exceeding the number of people who had attended the service. The tables were covered with paper tablecloths, water glasses standing ready to receive Nikos' *spitiko*, Benjamin and Adam rushing around adorning the tables with the plastic flowers they had retrieved from the *Dimarcheio*. The outdoor setting was perfect for the celebration, offering a stunning vista of sea views without any pesky sand to irritate Marigold.

Nikos had rigged up some kind of awning over the outside seating. By the looks of it he had fashioned the scruffy sun shade out of some old bed sheets, positioning it in place by hooking the corners around the branches of some convenient trees. The makeshift canopy was not aesthetically pleasing but the local strays seemed to appreciate it, dozing under the shade in sheer contentment.

Dina, having slipped a pinny on over her smart outfit, was busy carrying dishes of salads and dips out of the kitchen, with the help of Eleni and the village matriarchs I recognised as the same ladies that had relieved me of my outdoor bread baking duties.

"*Ela* Victor, what you to think of the canapé? I do the good job yes?" Nikos said by way of greeting, shaking my hand formally as though he hadn't seen me in weeks.

Glancing at the tables I could see no evidence of the canapés. Catching my perplexed expression Nikos waved grandiosely at the bedraggled bed sheets strung up above the tables. "I tell you I would to get you the canapé you want," Nikos said.

"That's actually a canopy," I corrected, thinking my description was more than generous.

"Yes, the canapé, it was the good idea you had to make the shade in the afternoon, yes, it is very the hot today," Nikos said with pride before striding off to check on the spit-roast lamb.

I couldn't help but chuckle, reflecting that the tatty 'canapé' didn't look very edible. If I'd wanted an actual canopy rather than canapés I would have told Nikos to fix up a *tholos*. Such a simple language mix-up meant that there would be no fancy canapés to impress our guests, but at least they wouldn't suffer sunstroke whilst tucking into the outdoor feast. Hoping that Cynthia wouldn't be too disappointed to be deprived of the promised posh finger food, I considered it was just as well her pretentious mother hadn't made it over to Greece. On the plus side when I popped indoors to answer a call of nature I was impressed to notice that Dina had given the facilities a thorough mopping and thrown a more than generous measure of bleach in the toilet.

Taking my seat between Barry and Marigold in the middle of one of the long tables, my stomach rumbled with anticipation as platters of delicious looking food began to pile up. Baskets of crusty bread and dishes of fat juicy Kalamata olives were dotted between huge bowls of fresh Greek salad and plates of *mizithra* and *manouri* cheese. A myriad selection of dips: *tzatziki, taramasolata, tirokafteri, melitzanosalata, pantzarosalata*, and *fava* graced the table, along with an assortment of *tyropitas* and *spanakopitas*, the tempting cheese and spinach pies still warm from the oven.

The mouth-watering aroma of lamb wafted over from the spit and Dina told us that the oven was full to bursting with *patates* roasted in *lemoni* and *rigani*. Nikos roped Guzim in to walk around topping up glasses from a five litre plastic bottle of *spitiko*, Nikos assuring me that he had put the best of his home made wine aside for a special occasion such as this. The Albanian shed dweller made the most unlikely waiter, though to his credit he did make an effort by flashing his toothless grin as he slopped wine into glasses.

Violet Burke made a song and dance of producing a beautifully wrapped wedding gift for the newlyweds. "At least she bothered, none of the Greeks have given them anything," Marigold hissed churlishly as Cynthia unwrapped six tins of Fray Bentos steak and kidney filched from my kitchen cupboards.

"You could always slip one into the oven here, they're a sight more tasty than the Greek idea of canapés, it's just more of their oily salads and olives," my mother said to Cynthia.

"We'll save the Fray Bentos for another time Vi, but I do love a tinned pie," Barry said appreciatively, earning a look from Cynthia that would have been withering if she wasn't so obviously elated to be a bride.

"Mother, it is high time you were adventurous and actually tried an olive," I dared her.

"You know I prefer a nice Tesco silver skin."

"Just try one olive, just one, it won't kill you."

"Go on, give it a try Granny," Benjamin urged.

"Ooh, actually it's a bit of all right. Pass me another one Victor, I could get quite a taste for them."

Everyone was seated and tucking into the delicious food with obvious relish. Before taking their own seats Dina and Nikos came over to congratulate the happy couple again, Dina telling Cynthia she was sorry it hadn't rained on her.

"But I'm glad it didn't rain," Cynthia said. "It would have ruined my hair."

"The Dina say the rain is the lucky for the wedding, it to symbolise the many children," Nikos said, tactlessly adding, "But I tell her the Cynthia is too the old to make the baby, *einai poly palia.*"

"*Den einai kan saranta,*" Dina contradicted her husband, telling him Cynthia wasn't even forty; Dina always did see the best in everyone.

Cynthia didn't respond, adjusting the heirloom veil to conceal her blushes. I felt for my new sister-in-law; sometimes our Greek friends could be blunt to the point of rudeness. Even though I shared Nikos' opinion I would never be tactless enough to voice it within earshot of Cynthia.

People began to arrive that hadn't attended the service, stopping by to say *na zisete* to the newlyweds, the traditional wish for a long life, before piling their plates up. Dimitris slipped Barry an envelope before having a quiet word in my ear, apologising for missing the service and confessing he couldn't bear to endure the collective noise of the car horns.

"Well you are here now, take a seat and enjoy the food."

"Thank you Victor, you are always sympathetic to my problem. I leave before the Nikos play the bouzouki, I cannot tolerate the music."

"I'm afraid the festivities might get quite loud later on when the dancing commences. My mother has some earplugs she could lend you if the noise carries to your house," I said, neglecting to mention said earplugs had already been on intimate terms with Violet Burke's eardrums. Whilst sharing earplugs is something I would personally never practice since I find the notion repulsively cringeworthy, there is actually very little risk of bacteria being spread through ear-wax.

"There's fifteen euros in this envelope," Barry hissed once Dimitris had moved on.

"Gosh that's very generous; perhaps Dimitris didn't have time to shop for a wedding gift so gave you money instead," I said.

"Victor, you must to know it is the Greek custom to give the money at the wedding," Spiros interjected. "Remember at the wedding of the Kostis and Eleni the Greeks give the money when they dance."

"I didn't realise it was an actual Greek custom," I said in surprise, recalling how Kostis had been rather taken aback to receive the gift of a toaster from me and Marigold. "I thought they'd just given money because they didn't have time to get to the shops in town."

"In England it is considered a tad vulgar to give cash as a wedding gift," Marigold told Spiros. "Many couples compile a wedding gift registry listing the things they'd like to receive, that way they don't end up with half-a-dozen woks but not a single toaster."

"I not to know what the wok is," Spiros said. "I not to understand your custom Marigold, why to tell the people what to buy? It is the easier all round to give the cash. Yes, the money is the better gift I think. You can to imagine every old woman to gift some gloomy icon..."

As if on cue Kyria Maria appeared at Barry's elbow, presenting him with a tissue wrapped object; discarding the tissue revealed a gloomy icon. It had a familiar look about it. On closer inspection I realised the icon was identical to the reproduction of the Lady of the Sign, Platytera, the gaudy icon we had inherited from Pedros' junk collection. Currently we used it to conceal the fuse box. I imagined the popularity of such icons being down to a job lot of them going cheap, perhaps flogged from the back of one of the roving vans selling brick-a-brack which put in periodic appearances in the village.

Staring at Cynthia hard Kyria Maria leaned in and snatched the veil from her head, warning *"prosektikos, tha parete tzatziki sto peplo."*

"What is she doing?" Barry shouted.

"She thinks Cynthia is going to get *tzatziki* on her veil. You can't blame her for being worried; it is a precious heirloom which holds special memories of her own wedding day."

Fortunately Cynthia didn't take offence, thanking the old woman profusely for lending her the special veil and telling her it had been an honour to wear it. Kyria Maria claimed the seat next to Violet Burke and in no time at all the two elderly ladies were talking away at each other companionably, each clueless to what the other was saying. Considering the language barrier I thought their knack of forging a friendship quite remarkable.

More people filed in as we ate, Giannis the handsome bee man, Litsa's garlic eating brother Matthias, Tina the shopkeeper, and a practical scrum of Meli pensioners. I recognised some of them as permanent features outside the shop, playing tavli in all weathers. Others I knew from my time cheffing in the taverna, some I was on nodding acquaintance with having run into them as they collected *horta* or tended their fields, still more I had never clapped eyes on before. To my surprise Cynthia and Barry were also both clueless to the identity of many of the gate-crashers, though they greeted them warmly when they came over to wish them *na zisete*. Since they were apparent strangers it was particularly touching to see them press envelopes containing five or ten euros onto the happy couple. I reflected that at this rate the wedding might prove quite lucrative for the newlyweds which would be very handy considering the amount they would need to spend to put their own mark on Harold's house.

Relative quiet descended when the platters of lamb and dishes of oven roasted potatoes were served, everyone eager to fill up on the scrumptious food. I reflected that Nikos may be totally useless when it came to canapés but he was nothing short of a master when it came to creating a succulent Greek feast. The peace was disturbed by a familiar voice booming "Hello yes beautiful towel, stinks yes." Smiling in amusement that Vasos had so adroitly expanded his English vocabulary, the addition of 'stinks' to his repertoire bringing his total lexicon to ten, I swivelled round to greet the *Kapetanios*.

I was literally gob-smacked at the sight of Vasos. He had clearly pulled out all the stops for the wedding. If not for his booming voice I wouldn't have recognised him; being so used to seeing him in the casual scruffs he wears on the boat I was shocked to see him saunter in clad in a dusky pink velvet blazer, a red and white polka dot silk cravat adorning his throat, a straw boater perched on his head at a jaunty angle. The overpowering scent of cheap aftershave preceded him, making me suspect he had doused himself in the nasty scent rather than actually bathing. Sami trailed in his wake, bizarrely wrapped up in a thick woollen jumper in spite of the July heat. Between them the two men practically carried Spiros' Uncle Leo, each of them having a tight hold on his elbows.

"*To vrikame sto dromo*," Vasos said, explaining they'd found Leo on the road.

"Spiros, it looks as though your uncle wandered off again," I called over.

Leaping up Sampaguita put her arm round the old man, leading him back to the table and making a general fuss of him.

"*Omorfo koritsi*," Vasos said, giving Sampaguita the once over. She did indeed look very pretty in her summer dress.

"*Anikei ston Spiro*," I said, making it clear that she belonged to Spiros before Vasos could get any ideas and declare his undying love.

Finally approaching the newlyweds Vasos managed to reign in his gushing compliments, no doubt reflecting that a woman's wedding may not be the appropriate moment to attempt to seduce her. Barry of course was an unknown quantity to Vasos since the pair of them had never met. Nevertheless Barry made a lasting impression; standing up to shake hands with the seafaring Romeo he drew himself up to his full height, saying "Hello beautiful towel, good to meet you at last."

My mother's ears perked up at Barry's words. Narrowing her eyes she struggled to place Vasos until it suddenly dawned on her that she'd met him on Pegasus. "Oh it's the towel man with the dirty yacht; I didn't recognise him with his clothes on."

Her words attracted a disapproving look from Norman who muttered something no doubt disparaging to his wife. Overhearing the slight, Benjamin piped up, "Neither did I Granny. Who'd have guessed the old seadog could carry off pink velvet with such panache?"

Vasos and Sami squashed themselves in next to Guzim and I noted with interest that before long the *Kapetanios* and the Albanian shed dweller were deep in conversation. Within minutes Spiros relayed a message to me, saying "the Guzim send to you the apology, he rude about the pink shirt being the homosexual. He say the *Kapetanios* tell him the pink is the fashion and the *Kapetanios* is much the success with the woman."

Chortling at the notion that Vasos' womanising ways could be described as successful, Marigold said, "The party is certainly a success, look how much everyone is enjoying the food. It might be a good idea if you gave your best man's speech now whilst everyone is still gathered round the tables."

"That's a good idea, it does seem to be an appropriate moment," I concurred, tapping my glass with a fork to gain attention. As the guests turned in my direction and chatter ceased, the sudden silence was disturbed by the ringing of a mobile phone. Papas Andreas looked at me apologetically before accepting the call. After listening to the caller for a moment he passed the mobile to Barry, saying "The Geraldine telephone to wish the *na zisete* to the happy couple."

"I suppose mobile calls have replaced the traditional method of sending a celebratory telegram," I said sarcastically.

"Really Victor, can you imagine how difficult it would be to have a telegram delivered out here in the sticks," Marigold said.

"It's a bit odd that she phoned Papas Andreas instead of Marigold, she's Marigold's friend," Cynthia said peevishly when Barry ended the call.

"I didn't bring my phone along today,"

Marigold said.

"Oh well I suppose it was nice of her to call and congratulate us," Cynthia conceded. "I was just a bit surprised as I rather thought that Geraldine had her eye on Barry."

"Surely you know that Geraldine has the hots for the Papas," I hissed, hoping to put the damper on Cynthia's jealous streak. "I expect she has his number on speed-dial."

"Your speech, Victor," Marigold reminded me.

"Of course," I agreed, reaching into my pocket for my speech and once again tapping my water glass to garner attention.

Groping around in my inside pocket for the papers my fingers brushed against the paper bag containing the pregnancy testing kit. I could hardly hand the delicate item over to Cynthia in full view of everyone. Looking at Cynthia it struck me that she didn't look sickly anymore; she was positively blooming with radiance. I reflected that her sickness that morning had most likely been down to bridal nerves and she had sent me on a wild goose chase to the pharmacy. The consensus appeared to be that the bride was the wrong side of forty, not that I would ever be so crass to ask, having been brought up to believe it impolite to quiz a woman about her age.

Opening the carefully penned paper to read out my masterpiece I was shocked to discover a fly in the ointment. Blushing furiously, it dawned on me that in my earlier haste to grab the speech I had inadvertently pocketed Milton's synopsis of 'Delicious Desire.'

Chapter 27

Woman's Work

B ravo Victor, *bravo*," Barry called out, prompting my rather baffled audience to break into applause. I could always count on my brother-in-law's support, even when I had just made a bit of a pig's ear of delivering the best man's speech.

"Really Victor, considering what a song and dance you made of supposedly perfecting your speech I was expecting nothing short of a work of literary genius," Marigold said disparagingly.

"I was caught unprepared when I discovered that I had pocketed Milton's explicitly saucy synopsis of his porn, rather than my own papers. Unfortunately I hadn't memorised my speech," I explained.

"You mean to say you had Milton's porn in your pocket," Barry guffawed. "You should have read it aloud and given us all a good laugh rather than trying to wing it with that feeble dirge."

"Don't be so unkind Barry; Victor's speech was perfectly adequate. I would have been mortified if he had read something smutty. I leafed through Milton's book and I think some of the elderly ladies here might have come down with a fit of the vapours if they heard something so racy."

"I doubt they're all such shrinking violets," Barry argued.

"Well I for one would have been embarrassed if Dad had read Milton's erotica in front of Granny," Benjamin said supportively. "Though I must say that joke about Dad being a bit smitten with the groom was really lame."

"I was forced to improvise at the last moment," I said in my own defence, a tad embarrassed that I'd resorted to repeating the bilge that I'd unearthed in my Google search.

"Well I thought it was lovely that you said my hair looked so glossy today," Cynthia gushed.

"Mentioning that Cynthia's teeth were glossy did seem a bit over the top though," Barry pointed out.

"And I was really touched by the way you welcomed me as part of your family, particularly as my own family aren't here for this special day," Cynthia said.

"You are part of the family now, for better or worse," Marigold said, squeezing Cynthia's hand.

Dina and her army of helpers began to clear the tables to make way for a veritable feast of sweet goodies, serving platters of tempting *galaktoboureko, baklava, bougatsa, loukoumades*, and *kourabiedes*. I decided that this would be a suitable moment to make my rounds of the tables since technically I was hosting the celebrations. Noticing that Tiffany appeared to be lacking company, I spotted Sakis entwined with a young woman I presumed was his girlfriend. Considering their coupling perhaps accounted for Tiffany's solitary state, I joined her, surprised to find her nibbling her way through a packet of digestive biscuits rather than tucking into the rich syrupy Greek confections.

"I don't want to like risk any of the food here after you told me how like filthy the kitchen is. I Googled E-coli and it sounds like really horrible," Tiffany explained. It appeared that the deliberate subterfuge I had employed to ensure my local taverna wasn't turned into an attraction for coachloads of tourists had made a lasting impression on the gullible rep. Not wishing to admit that I had deceived her, I explained away all the locals tucking into the food by telling Tiffany they had developed cast iron stomachs after years of coping with cockroach contaminated fare. It seemed cruel to confess I had duped Tiffany. There was no point in embarrassing her needlessly since she would be flying back to England as soon as Cynthia returned from her honeymoon.

"Those desserts do look like really good, but with you having been like a health inspector I know I can like trust you when you say they are a breeding ground for horrible nasty like bacteria," Tiffany said.

"Well if you have a sweet tooth why not enjoy these sugared almonds instead," I said, emptying my pockets of the *koufeta* I had scooped up from the steps outside the *Dimarcheio*. "I can promise you these haven't been anywhere near the filthy kitchen here." I felt a twinge of guilt watching Tiffany greedily devour the treats, but I reflected I had most likely pocketed them before any of the ferals had chance to give them a good licking.

After making the rounds of the other guests I returned to the family. Panos had joined Violet Burke, apparently enjoying her company and seemingly transfixed by the plastic cherries dangling from her hat as she talked at him. Adam was discussing the Olympic Games which were due to be hosted in Greece the following summer. Both Barry and Vangelis agreed that the Games would be good for their business, predicting that with Greece as the focus of the world's attention more foreigners would be inspired to move to our area.

"If there's an upsurge in English moving over it means more building work for us," Barry pointed out.

"Well I hope that not too many of them discover Meli, I rather like the village just as it is," I said. "I'd hate for it to be colonised by an army of ex-pats."

Whilst the others engaged in a conversation

about the merits of more foreigners moving to Greece, Barry took the opportunity to have a quiet word, asking how my book was coming along.

"Well naturally I haven't been able to get on with it with a house full of guests," I said. "I spent a lot of time on my best man's speech; sorry I let you down with that Barry."

"Don't be daft, it was fine, and at least you forgetting your papers meant that you kept it short. Nothing worse than a long speech that drags on endlessly."

"Perhaps the original was a tad wordy," I conceded.

"So will our wedding be featured in your book?" Barry asked

"Hardly Barry, I'm still at the stage of penning our first visit to the market. I'm sure any readers will appreciate my descriptions of such typically Greek scenes, after all my guided tour of the market went down a treat with the tourists."

"Perhaps you could pad it out with a cast of characters," Barry suggested. "I'm sure Cynthia would get a thrill seeing herself depicted in print, even if you do have to name change her."

"I can see through your game Barry, you're

just hoping to get a mention," I laughed, teasing him that he would need to wait until it was in print to find out if it featured his name-changed self. There was no way I was letting him near my work in progress after he had so wantonly fed the first copy into my shredder.

"What is Eleni doing?" Barry asked, watching as the young woman distributed small delicate net wrapped parcels in front of each guest.

"She's passing out the *bombonieres*," Marigold said, Barry's raised eyebrow prompting her to expand. "It is the Greek custom for the guests to receive a small gift of *koufeta*, sugared almonds. Each little parcel contains an odd number. Tradition decrees that any single women must place loose *koufeta* under their pillows; if they follow the tradition they will dream of their future husband."

"I'd best eat mine now then. The last thing I want is to be saddled with another husband at my age," Violet Burke spluttered through a mouthful of sugared almonds.

Nikos came over to join me, saying "Victor, I fetch the bouzouki to make the music, yes. We must to push the tables away to make the clear for the Greek dancing."

Nikos' words reminded me that I'd forgotten to have a quiet word with him about the Greek custom of breaking plates which I feared may get out of hand during the dancing. Although the custom is an integral part of such celebrations I was uncomfortable with the practice, aware that flying shards represented a very dangerous hazard. I imagined the custom must violate a number of safety regulations. I certainly didn't fancy running the risk of being sued by some litigious Greek who might suffer the misfortune of having an eye put out by a shard of flying ceramic. Having voiced my serious reservations to Nikos I was pleasantly surprised by his reaction.

"Victor, there will be no smashing the plate in my taverna. You think I am so the rich I let the customers break the plates when the Dina is the happy to wash them?"

"I just presumed that since it is the tradition..."

"The tradition for the fool with too much the money. You know the custom start from the braggart who like to demonstrate such the wealth he can afford to break the plate. Perhaps he so the ugly he not have the wife to wash the plate, eh Victor," Nikos said.

"The Junta ban the tradition back in the 69 because of the health and safety you are the always banging on about Victor," Spiros interjected. "I think the Junta just the joy kill."

"Killjoys," I corrected, relieved that I wouldn't need to dodge pieces of airborne plates after all.

"Some the people still do it, they spend the much money to buy the plaster plates to break," Nikos sneered. "I to think..."

We never got to discover what Nikos thought since he became distracted by the late arrival of the mayor. Some of the local pensioners practically mobbed the mayor as soon as they spotted him, demanding his attention. I surmised that he was either a very popular chap or he was suffering the complaints of every local who found it difficult to get to the *Dimarcheio* to voice their concerns about local politics, and perhaps I thought hopefully, the state of the rubbish bins.

Nikos called across to Eleni to rustle up a plate of lamb for the honoured guest. When Eleni didn't budge from her chair Nikos tutted "What is got into the girl, why she be so the lazy? It not like her, the Kostis marry the good worker."

Rather than plating up some lamb for the mayor himself, Nikos yelled out for Dina, telling her to get Eleni to do it. Dina sank into the chair next to Eleni, worry contorting her features. I watched as she tried to help Eleni to stand, but the younger woman collapsed back into her seat, groaning loudly.

"*Einai stin ergasia,*" Dina called over to Nikos.

"What did she say?" I asked Vangelis.

"She say the Eleni is in the labour," Vangelis replied as Athena rushed solicitously to Eleni's side. Other Greeks that had overheard began to run round like headless chickens, closing in around Eleni until she barely had space to breathe.

"She cannot to have the baby now, we have the wedding," Nikos complained. "I must to find the Kostis."

To my surprise my mother sprang into action, proclaiming "Don't panic, I'm perfectly capable of delivery a baby, there's nothing to it."

"I didn't know you had midwifery experience Vi," Marigold commented in surprise.

"Well not as such, but I nearly had to deliver a baby in the back of the chippy one time. The ambulance couldn't get through because of the waterworks."

"So you haven't actually ever delivered a baby," I clarified, recalling that Violet Burke had given birth to me in the back of a chippy.

"Well not as such, I'll grant you, but it was touch and go if the ambulance would get there in time," she admitted.

After conferring with his wife Nikos returned to tell us that his useless son Kostis was nowhere to be found. The mayor had graciously stepped in, offering to drive Eleni and Dina to the hospital since he had a large and comfortable car; it certainly struck me as a better option than expecting Eleni to hop onto the back of Nikos' moped. Dina took the time to come over and apologise to Barry and Cynthia for leaving the celebrations, saying she needed to be with Eleni to support her.

"Aren't you going with them?" Marigold asked Nikos.

"Bringing the baby is the woman's work; I must to stay to play the bouzouki for the dancing. I cannot to let Barry down."

As we gathered to wave Eleni off and wish her good luck I reflected it was most inconvenient that Kostis was not there to take his wife to the hospital: I would need to find another opportune moment to bend the mayor's ear with my innovative plans for bin sanitation.

Chapter 28

Dancing the Tsamiko

Most of the tables had been pushed to one side to clear a space for the dancing. The villagers were waiting with anticipation for Nikos to start playing the bouzouki. Everyone was in marvellous spirits, well lubricated from Nikos' *spitiko* and replete from having feasted on fabulous food. A round of applause erupted when Nikos struck the first cords of the *Tsamiko* wedding dance and Barry led his bride onto the improvised dance floor. When the music switched to the *Sirtaki* the bride and groom were soon surrounded by a bevy of dancing pensioners pinning money to them. Marigold and Doreen enthusiastically joined in with the dancing, showing off the moves they had picked up in their classes. My wife looked quite lovely, the emerald green dress showing off her trim figure, her Titian hair reflecting the sunlight, her carefree smile radiating infectious joy.

I stifled a laugh at the sight of Guzim attempting to master the complicated footwork, his right arm resting on Vasos' shoulder. It appeared the Albanian shed dweller was quite taken with the *Kapetanios*, though not of course in a homosexual way. Throwing an arm round my shoulder Benjamin joined me, pointing out Adam's attempts to keep pace on the dance floor with the ever nimble Kyria Maria. Unfortunately for Benjamin he had inherited my two left feet and felt more comfortable watching from the side-lines. Noticing Spiros spin Sampaguita around I wondered how long it would be until we celebrated their wedding, Spiros having hinted a proposal might be imminent since he believed his fragrant Filipina flower was destined to be his wife.

A tall stout woman with a brassy dyed blonde

hairdo pushed her way through the dancers, heading straight for me. I struggled to place her amongst the crowd of villagers. Realisation hit that it was Joan; I wasn't used to seeing Harold's unbearable wife clad in anything more than a transparent wrap over a bikini, but now she was fully clothed.

"Hello Vic, I've brought the keys over. I know you said to leave them in the shop but it was closed," Joan said apologetically. Catching sight of Tina doing some fancy footwork on the dance floor I realised Joan wasn't simply making an excuse to gate-crash the party.

"So you're all packed then?" I said.

"The van's just left, and I ran round with the hoover so it's all nice and clean, I know how particular you are."

"Very decent of you," I said. "So you didn't go in the van with your things?"

"No, Harold booked a taxi from town to take us to Athens; it should be here in about an hour. We didn't fancy sitting around in an empty house…"

"So where's Harold now?"

"He's waiting for me outside, he didn't like to intrude, you made it pretty clear he wasn't welcome," Joan said, embarrassment etched on her face.

"Nonsense, we can't expect the pair of you to wait in the street, bring him in for a drink," I invited, my previous antipathy towards the pair somewhat mellowed by my cheery mood. I reflected that they were hardly likely to get so plastered in less than an hour that I would rue my magnanimous gesture.

"I'm done in Vic, I think I'll head back to the house," my mother sighed, sinking wearily into a seat. The dancing was in full swing, the wedding guests making merry in the moonlight.

"You really threw yourself into the Greek dancing," I said admiringly. My mother had been quite a hit on the dance floor; it appeared that I must have inherited my two left feet from my father since Violet Burke had surprised me by being pretty agile for such a bulbous figure.

"I've always enjoyed a good bop, but I'll pay for it tomorrow, I expect my feet will swell up something terrible," she said, stifling a yawn.

"Come on, I'll walk you home," I offered.

"I can walk myself. You get back to the other young'uns."

Her words brought a smile to my face, but I supposed that in comparison to most of the villagers being labelled a youngster was quite apt. I decided that a walk would be pleasant and I could return to the celebrations after seeing my mother home.

"I'll walk you, I'd like to," I insisted, surprised to find I genuinely meant it. I mouthed "I'll be back" to Marigold in response to her questioning eyebrow when she saw us heading out.

Violet Burke linked her arm in mine for support as we strolled through the village towards home, the fragrant scent of lavender permeating the night air as we side-stepped the odd sleeping stray.

"I'm glad to get you on your own Vic, I've something a bit sensitive to bring up."

"Go on," I encouraged.

"Well you know how Benjamin came up to see me in Warrington...he went on a bit how you'd never known how you'd ended up in that bucket, but of course I've been able to put you right about that."

"I must confess it was a relief to finally hear the truth about how I came to be abandoned at the railway station," I admitted. I had come to terms with the circumstances leading to my abandonment, understanding how difficult it would have been for the young and penniless Violet Blossom to raise me with all the stigma associated with single motherhood. Things may have been different for her if she'd had the support of a loving family, but she was alone and penniless when the scoundrel that got her pregnant did a moonlight flit after getting wind that the military police were after him for going AWOL.

"Well Benjamin was saying how he'd have hated to grow up not knowing who is father was. You've done a grand job with that lad, a proper chip off the old block Vic...anyway he got me thinking and I did a bit of digging to see if I could dredge up anything about what happened to Vic after he did a runner."

"I must confess I have given a lot of thought recently to my paternity, wondering if my father is perhaps still alive and if he possibly spawned any siblings."

"He was definitely the type to go in for spawning, he had the gift of the gab did that one, a real charmer..."

"Did you manage to find out any information about him?" I asked impatiently.

"I got a few leads," she said. The pause seemed endless as I waited for her to continue.

"The thing is just before I flew out here I got word that he settled in Macclesfield. I've got an address for your father Victor, the old bugger hasn't croaked it, but he might if I get my hands on him."

"Are you sure it's him?"

"Pretty certain, I only got word a couple of days before I came here. If it hadn't have been all fixed for me to come out to Greece with the boys I would have got the train over to Macclesfield and confronted him."

Before I even had chance to let everything sink in, I made a spur of the moment decision. "I'll fly back with you Mum when you go back next week. We'll make the trip to Macclesfield together."

"Aye that makes sense Vic," my mother said, clamping my head to her bosom in a crushing embrace.

"Did you see your mother home okay?" Marigold asked when I returned to the taverna.

"Yes, she got back fine. She's soaking her feet in our washing up bowl and there's a Fray Bentos pie in the oven."

"She certainly seemed to enjoy herself today."

"It was a splendid day, but I'm ready for the off once Barry and Cynthia leave for their honeymoon. I had quite the chat with my mother and there's some things I need to discuss with you... but later when we're alone."

"We'll steal some private time on the roof terrace. Victor, whatever it is I'm here for you."

As Marigold spoke the bouzouki playing came to an abrupt halt. Clambering onto a chair Nikos called everyone to attention, announcing *"I Eleni eiche ena koritsi."* Upon hearing the news that Eleni had given birth to a baby girl everyone cheered, calling out *"Bravo"* when Nikos proudly added *"Eimai pappous,"* I am a grandfather.

"Have a Metaxa, Victor," Nikos offered, pouring me a generous measure to celebrate the birth of his granddaughter Nikoleta. In keeping with tradition the new-born had been named in honour of Nikos. His insistence on pouring me a drink that originated from a shop bought bottle, rather than his usual homemade wine, amused me. I was delighted to hear that Kostis made it to the hospital in time for the birth and could only imagine Dina's excitement.

"Barry, I hope the good news of the baby

not to rain on your parade," Nikos said.

"Not at all Niko, Cynthia and me are both delighted for you, and Meli could certainly do with some babies," Barry said. "It's been the most wonderful wedding day Niko, you have been a fabulous host, and Victor, you have been an amazing best man."

"Proud to do it," I said.

"We're going to push off now though, we've a honeymoon to get to," Barry announced with a broad wink, climbing into the van beside his new bride.

Everyone cheered and clapped as the van pulled away, trailing a string of ribbon-be-decked traffic cones from the bumper. I wondered whose bright idea it was to put Norman in charge of decorating the getaway car.

Chapter 29

The Wrong End of the Stick

Although the celebrations had continued late into the night, I found myself surprisingly full of energy the next day, just as well since there was the monumental task to face of knocking some kind of order into Harold's house before the honeymooners returned.

True to her word Joan had run round with the vacuum, though her idea of a hygienic home fell rather short of my exacting standards. The place looked strangely bare, bereft of the nasty purple shag-pile, though a lingering musty smell left me in no doubt that there was plenty of deep cleaning to do. Benjamin, Adam and my mother were by my side, keen to get down to the brass tacks of giving the place a good scrubbing, determined to have everything in pristine order before the honeymooners took up residence. Marigold was still at home, indulging in a rare lie-in.

Actually in truth Marigold's lie-ins are anything but a rarity. She had been so understanding the previous evening when I unburdened my fears about confronting my sweet-talking soap salesman father, that I feel the need to take poetic licence and write something to show how much I appreciate her enduring support. Little did Marigold expect when she agreed to marry an orphan that there would not only be one, but possibly two absconded parents of rather dubious pedigree, climbing out of the woodwork.

Benjamin and Adam volunteered to make a start on the upstairs bathroom. Barry had plans to rip out the enormous tub and replace it with a shower, but the renovations would take time. We all agreed that all trace of Harold and Joan would need to be scoured from the bath before Cynthia could enjoy a soak; no reasonable person could expect the newest member of our family not to baulk at any reminder of the previous occupants wallowing in it like a pair of beached whales.

Violet Burke didn't let a little thing like swollen feet stop her from getting stuck into scrubbing the kitchen. Armed with an industrial sized carton of Vim she made a start on the cupboards, exclaiming in surprise, "I thought you couldn't get this stuff over here Victor."

"What stuff is that Mother?" I called out, my head buried under the sink.

"Come and see, there's all sorts. I wonder how come they didn't take all this food back to England. It's a shocking waste to leave it all behind."

Peering over my mother's shoulder I was amazed to find the cupboards crammed to bursting with Fray Bentos pies, heaped packets of Vesta curries, almost a full case of Heinz baked beans, tins of alphabetti spaghetti, boxes of gravy granules, sage and onion stuffing mix, packets of Bird's custard powder and Angel Delight, tins of Spam, and box after box of Yorkshire teabags.

"Good grief, I didn't have Harold down as a hoarder," I said. "What's the date life on those

Vesta curries? I thought they stopped making them years ago."

"Oh look Victor, here's some Marmite. That will come in handy for you to ward off the mosquitoes; the foul stuff is fit for nothing else."

I exchanged a knowing look with my mother. Not only did we share a taste for Fray Bentos but we also shared a mutual loathing of Marmite.

"I wonder why they left it all behind, more money than sense," my mother said.

"It would have been like shipping coals to Newcastle. I think they are having their boxes shipped back to England, perhaps the cost of sending it all back was more than the value of the food," I suggested, thinking it must have cost them a small fortune to have imported it in the first place. It appeared from their hoard and the total absence of any Greek products that Harold and Joan must have spent their time in Greece eating exclusively British food. I reflected they were so set in their ways that it was little wonder they had failed to adapt to Greek life; if only they had embraced the new experiences and tastes on offer they may have lived a relatively content life in the village. Still their loss was Barry's gain and I couldn't see him complaining that he'd inherited a job lot of English grub. He would be sure to serve some garden grown veggies with the Fray Bentos to add a Greek spin to his plate. Perhaps he could donate the tins of Spam to Vasos.

Spiros arrived to disconnect the monstrous satellite dish that was such an eyesore, ready to cart it away to a discreet spot behind Leo's house so that Sampaguita could enjoy her favourite Filipino television programmes. He looked on with interest as Benjamin joined us in the kitchen carrying a box full of clutter he had retrieved from the bathroom cabinet.

"I think this lot is only fit for the bin Dad, there's nothing worth keeping hold of unless you happen to suffer from dandruff, haemorrhoids or constipation. Harold was stockpiling Alka Seltzer and bottles of Grecian 2000, Old Spice and Brylcreem."

"I take the Old Spice off your hand," Spiros offered, having inherited his uncle's weakness for collecting after shave.

"Has that Grecian 2000 been opened or is it still sealed?" I asked nonchalantly. I'd been unable to locate that particularly brand of hair dye in Greece and was a tad wary of experimenting with any product that only came with Greek instructions.

"The bin is the only place for these horrible damp budgie smugglers and this sticky bottle of fake tan. I don't suppose you've any use for this wart remedy?" Adam announced as he joined us, holding the offending articles at arm's length as though they would explode in his hand at any moment. It amused me to speculate who Harold had caught his warts from since he made a point of not mixing with the locals.

"Anyone fancy a brew? We may as well have a nice cup of Yorkshire," my mother offered, having come armed with our kettle so she wouldn't miss her elevenses.

The five of us gathered round the pool, sipping Yorkshire tea and munching our way through a packet of Mr Kipling cherry Bakewells that Violet Burke had unearthed in one of Harold's cupboards. I reflected that Harold had demonstrated a generosity I would not have expected from him in bequeathing his food stock; it would have been no skin off his nose to simply bin the lot out of spite considering how I had repeatedly spurned his friendly advances. At least I had made amends of sorts by inviting him to have a drink at the wedding.

Our quiet elevenses were interrupted by

Marigold steaming through to the pool, the look on her face enough to turn vinegar rancid.

"Victor a word in private now," she snapped in an icy tone, not even bothering to acknowledge the others.

Following Marigold through to the kitchen I felt a dire sense of foreboding. Something had clearly upset my wife and I had a sinking feeling that whatever it was must be my doing.

"You have some explaining to do Victor."

"How so?" I asked defensively.

"I thought I could trust you implicitly. In all these years of marriage I have never doubted you…"

"And I have never given you cause."

"What was it, was it moving to Greece? Was it finally being free of your work obligations? Did moving to another country make you feel younger and more attractive, and up for a dalliance? To think how quickly I dismissed Despina when she hinted you had another woman…"

"Marigold, I have never looked at another woman, you are the only one for me," I assured her, at a complete loss to fathom why my wife had apparently taken leave of her senses.

"Then perhaps you would like to explain how you managed to give some woman a pregnancy scare, Victor," Marigold demanded, flashing the pregnancy testing kit I had purchased for Cynthia under my nose. I must confess I had forgotten all about the test tucked into the inside pocket of my suit, having had no opportunity to slip it to Cynthia away from prying eyes.

"It is for Cynthia..."

"Victor, how could you, carrying on with your sister-in-law is practically incest? And poor Barry, cuckolded by you when he thinks of you as a brother. How could you?"

Two cups of Yorkshire tea and a cherry Bakewell later Marigold was still mortified by the baseless accusations she had flung at me, having accepted my account of the previous day's events and proffered a suitable apology. In a strident tone she said, "I think Cynthia must be delusional, there is no way she could be pregnant at her age; she's certainly no spring chicken and Barry won't see fifty again."

"Have you any idea how old she actually is?" I asked.

"Who knows, she's very vague on the subject. When I asked her bluntly she quipped that she was twenty one. I doubt even Barry knows."

"She may be younger than we think, is it really so far-fetched to suppose that Cynthia is pregnant?" I speculated.

"Cynthia is the pregnant, that is the wonderful news," Spiros said as he wandered in, having clearly eavesdropped on our private conversation.

"Of course she isn't, she is past it," Marigold said adamantly. "It is all in her head. It is perfectly natural for a bride to be overcome with nerves. Cynthia's bridal jitters made her feel queasy and she made the ridiculous leap to morning sickness. Anyway Barry has been sleeping on our sofa."

"And not just pretending to," I agreed.

"The Cynthia is not the past it, she is the only the age thirty nine," Spiros announced. "You must to know that."

"Well actually I never liked to pry, it is considered terribly rude in England for a man to ask a woman her age," I admitted.

"You English are the too polite to nose to the bottom of the everyone's business, but we Greeks like to cut to the chase and ferret the truth out. I know the age and the measurement of the everyone in the village," Spiros said, making me wonder if he'd acquired such knowledge with his coffins in mind.

Passing a cherry Bakewell to the self-pro-claimed omniscient undertaker Marigold patted the seat beside her, saying "Time to spill the beans Spiro, how old is Doreen really? And Norman, he tries to make out he's only sixty two but I've seen the Grecian 2000 in their bathroom."

Relieved that my wife was so easily dis-tracted I smiled fondly at her as she interrogated Spiros. Stepping outside I squinted at the swim-ming pool through the bright sunlight, trying to imagine how it would look transformed into a weed infested ecological pond complete with floating lily pads, frogs and water stick insects. Perhaps inspired by Nikos' 'canapé' I could rig up some kind of sunshade; after all if my inkling was correct it would be a lovely spot to park a pram. Once Marigold got used to the idea, she would be tickled pink to be an aunt.

Our adventures in Greece didn't end here. You can read more of our exploits in continuing volumes of the Bucket saga.

A Note from Victor

All Amazon reviews most welcome.
Please feel free to drop a line if you would like
information on the release date of future volumes in the Bucket series at
vdbucket@gmail.com

Printed in Great Britain
by Amazon